D1575438

Narrative and structure

Narrative and structure: exploratory essays

JOHN HOLLOWAY

Professor of Modern English in the
University of Cambridge
and Fellow of Queens' College

CAMBRIDGE UNIVERSITY PRESS
Cambridge
London · New York · Melbourne

Published by the Syndics of the Cambridge University Press
The Pitt Building, Trumpington Street, Cambridge CB2 1RP
Bentley House, 200 Euston Road, London NW1 2DB
32 East 57th Street, New York, NY 10022, USA
296 Beaconsfield Parade, Middle Park, Melbourne 3206, Australia

© Cambridge University Press 1979

First published 1979

Phototypeset in V.I.P. Bembo by
Western Printing Services Ltd, Bristol
Printed in Great Britain at the
University Press, Cambridge
Library of Congress Cataloguing in Publication Data

Holloway, John.
Narrative and structure.

1. Narration (Rhetoric) – Addresses, essays, lectures. I. Title.
PN212.H6   808.3   78–20826
ISBN 0 521 22574 4

CONTENTS

PN
212
H6

459488

PREFACE

The main part of this book comprises five chapters on various aspects of narrative structure, and various works of fiction which have seemed to me to elucidate them. In some of these chapters certain mathematical ideas make an appearance, but I should be the first to hope that others, better qualified than I, may see possibilities of advance far beyond what I have attempted.

The topics or works I have selected have been selected for a particular reason. I do not think it would have been fruitful to confine the book to, say, fiction from a certain historical period, or by some certain author. If that had been the method adopted, the likelihood is that some of the works might readily have lent themselves to the kinds of analysis attempted here, and others much less so. The probable result would have been laboured, artificial and unrewarding. Still less, I believe, would it have been wise to plot out varieties of analysis in the abstract, and then cast about for narratives to subject to them.

Instead of either of these ways of proceeding, I have waited until I found works that, on reflection, looked as if they raised particular problems in the field of a certain kind of analytic approach, or would perhaps make it fruitful in their particular case. The first five chapters, therefore, are a series of fresh starts only superficially. Essentially, they try to explore a large field by opening it up at the points where it most invites exploration, because a way of thinking, and a literary work, seem to come together promisingly.

The concluding chapter tries not so much to draw the threads together (I believe that, again, would have produced something fruitlessly abstract and 'programmatic'), but to assess some of the ways in which these various kinds of analysis bear upon the most central concerns of criticism, the 'nerve and life' of the critic's task. The two appendices, one mainly on poetic structures, the other on oratory, are included because their methods of enquiry are clearly analogous to those in the main chapters, on narratives. What is offered to the reader in all, therefore, is a book which does not circumscribe and conclude a discussion, though I hope it opens one.

Chapters 1 and 5 are revised versions of essays that appeared first in *Critical Inquiry* (in 1976 and 1975 respectively); Appendix 1 was published in *Miscellanea Anglo-Americana: Festschrift für Helmut Viebrock*, Munich, 1976; and Appendix 2 in George Levine and William Madden (eds), *The Art of Victorian Prose*, 1968. For all these grateful acknowledgement is made here. A number of colleagues in Cambridge and also Manchester Universities have discussed ideas in this book with me, and I now offer them thanks.

Cambridge, 1979   J.H.

1

Supposition and supersession: a model of analysis for narrative structure

I

The first and preliminary part of this chapter examines Todorov's remarks, in his article 'Structural Analysis of Narrative' (*Novel* 3, no. 1, Fall, 1969), on certain tales in the *Decameron*. These are advanced as dealing with a 'concrete problem' which 'illustrates' what Todorov 'conceive[s] to be the structural approach to literature'. The second part (sections II–V) offers an alternative analysis of the *Decameron* tales. The third part comprises some observations, from a similar point of view, on *Crime and Punishment*. The anterior purpose of the whole discussion is to identify at least some points where insights about 'structure', in a fairly strict sense, seem to bear genuinely upon the insights of the literary critic.

Todorov considers four *Decameron* tales in his essay: day 1. tale 4, day 9. tale 2, and day 7. tales 1 and 2. The first pair are about nuns or monks with lovers, the second pair about wives with lovers. 'It is easy to recognize that these four plots . . . have something in common', he says. He endeavours to 'express that' by means of a 'schematic formulation' which displays what is common to the four plots. This common something is expressed as a series of 'actions', put in generalized terms. Todorov acknowledges an extent of difference between the first two tales, where the key point in both narratives is that 'authority' proves to be as guilty as the culprit; and the second two, where the key point is that 'authority' supposes the culprit not to be a culprit at all. He therefore offers alternative statements of the fourth 'action' in the sequence of actions common to all the tales. His total account (the spatial arrangement below I believe clarifies Todorov's interpretation rather more than he clarified it himself) runs as in table 1. Todorov annotates and expatiates a good deal, but this is the core

Table 1

	Action no.		
	1		X violates a law
entails	2		Y must punish X
entails	3		X tries to avoid being punished
entails	4	either	Y violates a law
		or	Y believes that X is not violating a law
entails	5		Y does not punish X

of his account as to the essence of the findings of the 'structural approach to literature' in this case.

It must be conceded that this account falls short of adequacy. First, the above is barely 'structure' of narrative, because it is too near to summary of narrative. To talk about structure is to talk about form *in the sense that what one says can be formalized:* which means that it can in principle be expressed in a formal notation, a symbolism. Thus Propp's discovery about the Russian folk-tales he analysed[1] may be expressed by saying (1) that the events in any such folk-tale are a subset of a basic set; (2) that a sequential relation holds between any two events in the basic set; and (3) that every ordered pair of events in any existing tale must reappear as such in the basic set. That was the core of Propp's discovery, and it related wholly to form. The same cannot be said of Todorov's analysis, and I do not see how it could be generalized so as to be stated formally without becoming vacuous.

Second, the analysis is imperfect in that it effectively elucidates neither the structural similarity, nor the structural difference, between the first pair and the second (wife/husband) pair. To be sure, the two pairs are, as Todorov says, alike. But the structures of all four do not in the least look identical. On mere inspection, the two members of each pair are more like each other than either is like either member of the other pair; and if analysis of the likeness does not, almost of itself, throw up an account of the difference also, it is likely enough to be inadequate even over likeness. This problem will be resumed in section IV below.

The third point is surely the decisive one. Todorov envisages the relation between individual actions (as he calls them) to be one

1. V. Propp, *Morphology of the Folktale*, transl. L. Scott (2nd edn, University of Texas, 1968).

of *entailment.* Certainly, this is nearer the truth than to think of them as one simply of *sequence.* Clearly the relation to be identified is not that of sequence ('occurs subsequently to') alone, because the whole point and interest of these stories (as of almost any) is that each 'action' is somehow 'called out' or rendered appropriate, or something of that kind, by its immediate predecessor (or more truthfully, by all its predecessors collectively). On the other hand, there is certainly not an entailment relation. To say '*a* entails *b*' is to say 'if *a* then not-possible not-*b*'. Self-evidently, no such relation, or anything like it, holds between actions 2 and 3 in Todorov's sequence (see table 1), nor between his actions 3 and 4. Mere inspection is enough to show the suggestion for an extravagance. The matter need not be pursued.

More important is the fact that no entailment relation can be thought to hold between actions 1 and 2, or 4 and 5. I will not appeal to Hume's exposure of attempts to argue from *is* propositions to *ought* propositions, though I note in passing that propositions such as 2 are for the most part entailed by several propositions together, not just one. But the fact is simply that entailment is not a characteristic relation between contiguous narrative events. To think it is so is to suppose that the narrative *could not possibly* take a turn other than what it does, that there could not possibly be a narrative beginning with Todorov's 'action' 1 that does anything other than proceed through 2, 3, and 4 to terminate at 5. No one believes that. We know at once that the matter is otherwise. We also know surely, with a like immediacy though for quite other reasons, that 'action' 4 in these tales is not 'entailed' by action 3 (nor by actions 2 and 3, nor 1, 2, and 3 if it comes to that). Here the relation seems to be different from that between 1 and 2: but even more clearly, it is not entailment.

II

These two facts bring the discussion to its first point of real interest. What sort of relation do we in fact see between 'actions' 1 and 2, or 3 and 4, once we have set ideas of entailment aside? There appear in fact to be two more or less contrasting relations. For that between 1 and 2 in Todorov's analysis the Scots word *propone* seems to be appropriate. *To propone* is to 'propose for consideration, acceptance, or adoption' (*OED*). To say that a monk has violated a law *brings up the matter* of his abbot's punishing him. This does not mean that it is not possible for the abbot not to do so, nor that he will do so, nor anything of the kind. Nor will it do to say that it 'creates an expectation . . .', though that is certainly nearer the mark. Narrative expectations are determined not only by the items of the narrative but also – and more – by the whole context of the narration, and are a complex and dubious matter. The title heading of *Decameron*, 'Day Two' ('si ragiona di chi, da diverse cose infestato, sia oltre all sua esperanza *riuscito a lieto fine*') in fact makes us confidently expect, for example, that in these tales abbot will *not* punish errant monk. But action 1 above certainly raises the possibility of punishment. It proposes that for acceptance or adoption. To narrate 1 is, we may say, to 'propone' 2. We might call 2 a 'proponition' if we were drawn towards coining terms. I propose instead to call such an item, more simply, a 'supposition'. Todorov is right to speak of its 'modality'. The exact status of the suppositions which make part of any narrative warrants further elucidation. Suppositions, one may note, do not arise in a narrative only in respect of (to put the matter inadequately) events which do not happen. Rather, they arise all the way through, and in quantity. Then, as a regular thing there is a supposition of some event X which is fulfilled or realized if X eventuates. These four stories will illustrate that. When the reader finds in the first pair that the abbot or abbess also has a lover, he is at once disposed to think something more or less like 'then no doubt he (she) will have to let him (her) off' – that is, there is a supposition that (5), and thus the story is that (5) eventuates. It may be helpful at this point, incidentally, to distinguish what I might call minor suppositions, which relate to what the characters will do or say *next*, for example, and major suppositions, which relate to the outcome and resolution of the whole tale. It is the latter which concerns the rest of this chapter.

The relation between Todorov's 3 and 4 is something else. Here, there is not the faintest hint of 'entailment' (to revert to that misnomer). So far from that, we have the sense, at any such point in a work, that the narrative is taking a quite new turn: as if the last thing we should expect about, say, a nun who was involved with a lover would be that her abbess would be involved with a lover too. This is only a prima facie way of looking at the matter: as we become familiar with the *genre*, our expectations are probably reversed, and we must remember that 'expectations' is anyway not the right word for the reading experience. The question, here as elsewhere, is in fact of what the narrative 'propones': of the suppositions that it progressively puts forward for acceptance or adoption. At every stage in the action some new one is being added or some of the established ones eliminated. The reading experience, at least for narratives like those of the *Decameron*, is created within what might be termed the system of *two sets or series:* the series of events (Todorov's 'actions') on the one hand, and the suppositions which generate and proliferate along with these. Thence come the intrigue and suspense of the narrative.

To say that the suppositions proponed by the narrative are numerous is probably true in all cases and certainly in some. But in the *Decameron* tales analysed by Todorov in his article the suppositions are only numerous if we have regard to the minor suppositions. With regard to suppositions relating to the resolution and outcome of the tales, there are on the whole *only two:* and it is at this point that we reach matters about structure which may be expressed in formalized terms but which are of genuine interest from a literary standpoint.

Speaking in broad terms, we may say that narratives comprise (1) events which happen in (2) states of affairs: neither (1) nor (2) is sufficient to make up a narrative by itself. In the *Decameron* tales, we recurrently find an opening section which establishes a state of affairs, and then this is followed by something of quite another kind, something that constitutes the first significant event of the story. Let us call this event the *initiating event* of the narrative (e_i). The key fact about it is not that it is the *first* event in the tale (events may occur in the preliminary section, that which establishes the initial state of affairs) but that it is the first item of any kind in the narrative to *propone a supposition* in the sense explained above. Hence its significance.

Tales 7.2 and 9.2 follow rather similar and rather conspicuous patterns in their earlier stages. What is meant by that may be shown, briefly, by summary as follows. In 7.2 there is an initial preliminary set establishing the first state of affairs: the poor mason who lives in Naples and has a 'bella e vaga giovanetta' as wife. This story sets up a small social group, a sub-society, established in a stable way of life; and it uses the appropriate grammatical marker as regards tense in doing so. 'La lor vita *reggevano* come *potevano* il meglio.' The initiating event then follows, however, and replaces the past continuous tense by the past definite. '*Avvenne* che un giovane de' leggiadri . . . s'inna-morò di lei.' Something of a new stable society is created once the 'giovane' becomes the lover and joins her in the house of a morning as soon as he sees the husband go off for the day. 'Cosi *molte volte* fecero.'

There then comes a second event of consequence. One morn-ing the husband returns ('a casa se ne tornò'). In 9.2 the prelimi-nary set ('Sapere . . . dovete in Lombardia essere un famosissimo monisterio . . . nel quale . . . v'era una giovane . . . ,' etc.) is once again followed by the initiating event that the 'giovane' *'s'inna-morò'* with a handsome young man, who then visits her 'occultis-simamente . . . *non una volta ma molte*'. Once again, something approaching a new but stable order is established: what happens not once but many times over propones no supposition about the future save perhaps that it will happen more times still – and there would be nothing to narrate. That is not the situation however, '*avvenne* una notte che egli . . . fu veduto'. There occurs, that is, a second event of consequence much like that in 9.2.

The narrative of 1.4 is somewhat more condensed, but the same pattern of preliminary set ('era un monaco', etc.), initiating event (*'fa* accordato con lei e seco nella sua cella ne la menò'), and significant second event (*'avvenne* che l'abate . . . sentì lo schiamazzìo') may be identified, and of course in each case the significance of these second events – that the husband returns unexpectedly, the young man is seen, the abbot hears the commo-tion – is that they also each propone a supposition which is somehow the contrary of that proponed by the initiating event. That event, each time, proponed the termination of a stable state for a certain social group and its replacement by another con-dition. The second event, hereafter called the *reversing event* (e$_r$), propones, in some form, the termination of what the first in-itiated.

III
If tale 7.2 is considered more closely, it transpires that the polarity set up by these two events is sustained repeatedly by the detail of the narrative. For convenience I summarize this below (see table 2). Such a narrative may be seen in terms of a fairly sharply defined structure constituted by (1) *relations between the events of the narrative* and (2) *relations between the suppositions they propone*.

Table 2

Event in the narrative	Propones the supposition
Husband returns unexpectedly, finds door locked, knocks, gets no answer.	Wife's illicit love affair will be discovered (A).
Husband praises wife's honesty for locking door.	*Converse* of (A): the love affair will not be discovered (Ā).
Wife is obliged to admit husband while lover hides (in a barrel) in the same room.	(A)
Wife takes initiative and complains of husband's idleness in returning.	(Ā)
Husband says, on the contrary, he has found a purchaser *for the barrel*.	(A)
Wife says she already has one, at a higher price.	(Ā)

This may be the moment to introduce a complication which would render the discussion more exact; though for the most part, having mentioned it, I shall ignore it in order to avoid cumbrousness of expression. Strictly speaking, what in any narrative propones a supposition is not an individual item in the narrative but the *total* of items up to and including that one. What will be said about narrative structure in the rest of this discussion will be based throughout on the model of thinking of a narrative not as one set of events but as a *set of sets:* each member of this total set is a set of events which represents the narrative *so far as we have read* (or listened) *up to a certain point in it*. The distinction is fundamental, and it seems to me to conform significantly to our actual reading experience. We read, say, sentence (n) of the narrative and have a certain sense of that as a whole, *so far*. Then we ready sentence ($n + 1$), and form a new total sense; likewise again when we have read sentence ($n + 2$). A diagram (of a narrative with five events, as in Todorov's analyses) may clarify this (see table 3). Strictly speaking, the proponing relation relates a line in

Table 3

1. Successive events in the narrative	2. Successive narrative sets in the reading	3. Supposition Proponed by a set
e_1	e_1	
e_2	e_1 e_2	
e_3	e_1 e_2 e_3	A
e_4	e_1 e_2 e_3 e_4	$\bar{A}$
e_5	e_1 e_2 e_3 e_4 e_5	A

column 2 with an item in column 3, though in the discussion which follows the terminal item alone will usually be cited. Narrative structure is being considered here not in terms of column 1 (which represents the *text*, not the structure of the text) but by what may be said of the set of sets constituted by the total contents of column 2, line by line.

In these narratives there appear to be two major suppositions: they are proponed, respectively, by the initiating event and the reversing event – or rather, to speak once again more strictly, by the items comprising the narrative up to and including the former of these, and by the same up to and including the latter. At this point, one can perhaps begin to indicate the structure, in a mathematical sense of that word, of such narratives as these; and in doing so recognize how this has interest for literary study.

To begin with, we can see the structure of such a narrative as not a single set of event-items but as a set of sets or rather series of sets, each greater than its predecessor by one item, and each representing our sense of the narrative as we read it progressively on. We shall have the set of event-items $\{e_1 \ldots e_i\}$, say, where the event (e_i) is the initiating event. That set, therefore, will be the first to propone a supposition. Somewhat further on, our reading up to a later part of the narrative will supply the set $\{e_1 \ldots e_r\}$ where (e_r) is the reversing event, and this will be the first set to *propone the converse* of the supposition proponed by the set $\{e_1 \ldots e_i\}$.

Both of these suppositions, we should note, relate in fact to a *final term* in the series of sets, to how the narrative will resolve and conclude: either the lovers will continue indefinitely to meet 'molte volte' ('and if they have not left off, they are feasting still', to recall a familiar narration marker for a certain type of tale resolution), or, there is a last time, and part of the resolution of the narrative is that they do not meet again.

The structure of narrative may now be further articulated from the summary schema offered above for *Decameron* 7.2; for here, the set $\{e_1 \ldots e_r\}$ propones the supposition A, the set $\{e_1 \ldots e_{r+1}\}$ propones the converse (call it Ā), the set $\{e_1 \ldots e_{r+2}\}$ propones A once again, and so on. Since in no case is it the last item, in isolation and by itself, which propones the new supposition, but rather the new member in the series of sets, we may regard the fact that such-and-such a set propones A (or Ā) as *a relation between the members of that set*. Thus, the members of the set $\{e_1 \ldots e_r\}$ are related by an r-adic relation[2] by virtue of which they propone A, the set $\{e_1 \ldots e_{r+1}\}$ by an $(r + 1)$-adic relation by virtue of which they propone Ā, and so on. It should be noted that of the two suppositions proponed, one is a stasis and the other is the opposite: we might say, cataclysmic. One perpetuates a social order, the other violates or terminates it. Which is which, is not constant from tale to tale. The matter is one way round in the 'molte volte' narrations, the other in the others: and this indicates a significant difference in structure between narratives like 1.4, and narratives like 7.2 and 9.2, where the disruption of social order itself becomes a matter of 'molte volte' and thus a kind of new order.

We are now in a position to set out such a structure schematically. This structure comprises a series of sets, each one greater than the last by one item (the new item, the 'next step' in the tale as we call it); and each proponing, alternately, the supposition A or Ā. We may set this out, calling to mind the idea that the set $\{e_1 \ldots e_r\}$ propones by virtue of an r-adic relation between the n members and so on, and treating the reversing event as (e_r) where $(r - i)$ may $= 1$, as in table 4, and so on. The structure of the whole is then represented by the entire *series* of these relational propositions. On reflection, however, we may simplify this. For if we consider on the one hand what is to be understood by these i-adic or r-adic relations, we see that all we know about them is that they are what makes $\{e_1 \ldots e_i\}$ propone A, $\{e_1 \ldots e_r\}$ propone Ā, and so on; and if we consider, on the other hand, what we understand by A or Ā, it seems to me – I am not very sure about this – that we mean simply that the whole narrative has one last term (like 'and the lovers never met again') or another (like 'and if they have not left

2. An r-adic relation being simply a relation between r items or elements, as a diadic relation is a relation between two, triadic between three, etc.

Table 4

$\{e_1 \ldots e_i\}$	R_i	A	(The events up to and including the *initiating* event propone . . .)
$\{e_1 \ldots e_r\}$	R_r	$\bar{A}$	(The events up to and including the *reversing* event propone a contrary outcome.)
$\{e_1 \ldots e_{r+1}\}$	R_{r+1}	A	
$\{e_1 \ldots e_{r+2}\}$	R_{r+2}	$\bar{A}$	

off, they are doing it still') – whether these are explicit or merely implied making no difference. Therefore, the structure may be stated more simply by thinking of a *single* relation between members of the successive sets (that pointed to, in our common readers' parlance, by an expression like 'at this stage it looks as if . . . *will* . . .') and by treating the two suppositions as two alternative possible terminal sets – that is, total narratives. By that expression is meant the narrative as we shall have it on concluding our perusal of it (not of course its structure, but merely its contents). We then have the structure of such a narrative represented by a series of sets of the kind in table 5: the *structure* of the whole narrative still being represented by the entire series of these relational propositions.

IV
　　This kind of analysis strikes me as apposite to the most striking literary qualities of the tales: their basic simplicity (for the structure indicated above, though elaborate, may in fact be seen to be relatively simple); their constant stimulation of the reader's curiosity as to outcome; and the binary, yes–no nature of that curiosity. It also enables us to indicate a structural distinction between the two monastery tales (1.4, 9.2) and the two marital tales, which is obvious enough in fact, but of which Todorov had nothing to say. This distinction may be elucidated if we consider more closely the preliminary set of items as indicated above (p. 5). For if this preliminary set consists of the item $\{e_1 \ldots e_{i-1}\}$ – the items, that is to say, up to but not including the initiating event – then it is clear that in every narrative there are many items in the preliminary set which are not explicitly stated but which the

Table 5

$\{e_1 \ldots e_i\}$	R	$\{e_1 \ldots e_{z1}\}$	(e_1 is the *initiating event*)
$\{e_1 \ldots e_r\}$	R	$\{e_1 \ldots e_{z2}\}$	(e_r is the *reversing event*)
$\{e_1 \ldots e_{r+1}\}$	R	$\{e_1 \ldots e_{z1}\}$	
$\{e_1 \ldots e_{r+2}\}$	R	$\{e_1 \ldots e_{z2}\}$	

reader is called upon to take for granted. If he does not take for granted that husbands will be sexually jealous, tales 7.1 and 7.2 will simply have no point for him. They will never even begin to engage his attention or curiosity (save, I suppose, insofar as they do so not as narratives at all but as documents which are simply incomprehensible cultural oddities). Similarly he must take for granted that abbots and abbesses will object to their subordinates having lovers. Without that, tales 1.4 and 9.2 would also have no suspense and no point. But in respect of these two tales there is another necessary assumption: that the head of 'un monistero . . . di santità e di monaci più copioso che oggi non è' (1.4) or 'un famosissimo monistero di santità e di religione' (9.2) will himself or herself be chaste; in these two tales, the reversal event (e_r) is simply the denial of that item in the preliminary set. In tales 7.1 and 7.2 the counter event is not such a denial at all: it is an item proponing the supposition that someone (namely the husband) *will come to know* of the initiating event – and therefore, the further supposition that the resolution of the narrative will be of the 'never again' kind rather than its contrary. This difference between tales 1.4 and 9.2 as against 7.1 and 7.2 can be indicated fully by means of symbolism and so must be a structural difference.

There is something else which is a matter of the structure of these narratives and about which Todorov says nothing – of which his analysis in fact could say nothing. One may approach this in general terms by saying that the four narratives Todorov analyses are all much more pointed and witty than his analysis recognizes. To a greater or lesser extent, each narrative inclines us to chuckle gleefully. We feel that something like the same thing is prompting us to this in each case; and since there is nothing like an identity of content, the effect ought to be related not to content but to structure (form). Disregarding this aspect of the question is what led to a step in Todorov's analysis of tales 1.4 and 9.2 that was both lame and tame. ' "Y violates a law" entails "Y does not punish X" ' is really no good. We know in general that 'a sinner does not punish a sin' is more often false than true. What was it that made it impossible, or nearly so, for abbot or abbess in those tales to punish erring monk or nun? Todorov has not identified it, yet it is something like the essence of both of these narratives. Without it they would simply bore.

I have suggested that two events in these narratives have already transpired as of special importance: the initiating event which is the first to propone a supposition as to outcome and the reversing event which is the first to propone the opposite or counter supposition to that. A third especially significant event must also be identified, and I shall call it the *terminating event:* because although it may well not be what comes in the very last place in the narrative (and so not strictly be *terminal*), it is indeed what resolves the narrative and finally determines its conclusion, everything that follows it being mere consequence and detail. Important, however, is that it is this terminating event which appears to embody and release the point and wit of the narrative.

Other witty moments doubtless occur. In tale 1.4, for example, the abbot, when in his turn he has the girl that he finds in the monk's cell, is concerned about her 'tenera età' and his own 'grave peso' (or, the story says ironically, this was perhaps the explanation) and so had intercourse with her *in modo incubi* rather than in the allegedly more usual position. Doubtless this makes the reader smile. But what makes him laugh and sets 1.4 altogether apart from Todorov's trite ' "Y violates a law" entails "Y does not punish X" ' is that later, when the abbot begins to reprove the monk, the latter's reply is a witty exploitation of the fact that he has observed the abbot's activities through the keyhole. 'Voi ancora non m'avevate mostrato che i monaci si debban far dalle femine . . . ma ora che mostrato me l'avete, vi prometto . . . di mai più in ciò non peccare, anzi farò sempre come io a voi ho veduto fare ([You did not show me before now how a monk ought to comport himself in respect of a woman . . . but now that you have done so, I promise you . . . never to be at fault over this again, since I shall always act after your example]': some English translations entirely miss the witty irony of 'peccare' here). It is with these words that there emerges the central and essential wit of the tale, as opposed to its incidental witticisms. It occurs as the narrative is in effect resolved and terminated; and the crucial point is that this terminal event is made possible, as regards its detail, by the detail of the earlier event.

In these tales, in fact, it is the regular thing for the *terminating* event to have wit and point and to gain it precisely from how it resumes and exploits an earlier event – often the reversing event itself. In tale 9.2 the abbess is told her novice is in bed with a man, when she herself is in bed with the abbot. In her haste, she puts the abbot's underpants on her head instead of her coif. When she begins her reprimand, the novice answers 'first put your head-dress to rights and then you can scold me as much as you like'. (Collapse of abbess.) In tale 7.2 the husband comes home *to sell the barrel:* the terminal event is that the matter of selling the barrel is what makes consummation of the lover's illicit amour possible once again after all. In tale 7.1 the simpleton hymn-singing husband himself gives warning to the lover by singing the orison his wife teaches him for that very purpose.

If these details are set out in tabular form, a simple conclusion suggests itself (see table 6). It is, that the wit of the terminating event lies each time in its dexterous resumption and modulation of earlier events. In the first three of those narratives, what takes place is something like an amalgam of the reversing event and the initiating event. In tale 7.1, there is something like an amalgam of the reversing event and a major item of the preliminary set. In each case, the earlier events can readily enough be inferred from the terminating event, though (save perhaps by those for whom over-diligent study has spoilt the fun) not vice versa. In the first three cases, in fact, we can represent this further element of structure by a sort of equation, and write:

$$e_t = f(e_i, e_r)$$

The neatness of the tales, indeed, seems to reside in how the terminating event rearranges the perspective in which we see the reversing event. But what this means is that the reader now sees that event as proponing, after all, the supposition A, and not $\bar{A}$, as at first (see above, p. 8). If the husband of an unfaithful wife comes home and disturbs the lovers in order to sell a *barrel* (this is the clearest case, as it is in my opinion the neatest and wittiest tale) he is asking for more trouble. If the erring abbot adopts an unusual position for his own escapades, if the irate abbess puts on

Table 6

Preliminary set Includes	Initiating event (e_i)	Reversing event (e_r)	Terminating event (e_t)
1.4	Monk's illicit intercourse	Intercourse *in modo incubi*	Monk undertakes to have *illicit intercourse only in modo incubi*
9.2	Nun's illicit intercourse	Underpants for coif	Nun excuses *illicit intercourse* by reference to *underpants for coif*
7.2	Illicit intercourse	Selling the barrel	*Illicit intercourse* while *selling the barrel* (i.e., to the lover)
7.1	Husband sings 'orazione'	Illicit intercourse	Lover's untimely knock	*Lovers' untimely knock* leads to warning by *husband's 'orazione'*

a man's underpants for her coif when she hurries away to exact vengeance, they are only smoothing the paths of their scandalous subordinates. Or again, the posturing hymn-singer of a husband who has 'una bellissima donna e vaga per moglie' is arming her against himself by that hymn-singing alone, and from the start. These are the altered perspectives that the terminating events impose upon earlier ones (and especially the reversing event) in resuming and amalgamating them. But the point, so far as structure is concerned, is that the terminating events stand in certain formal relations to prominent earlier items in the series (particularly, in these narratives, to the reversing event items), and that they therefore stand in formal relations also to the suppositions that those propone.

V

To some considerable extent, it seems as if there may well be a structure in the genuinely mathematical sense in the Boccaccio tales. This transpires if we think of the *set of events* in the narratives – the members of this set being related by a relation of succession, in that they all come one after another – and along with that the set of *suppositions* generated by those events in the manner indicated above. It appears that these two sets satisfy the mathematical condition for a *morphism;* with immediate *succession* as the operative relation between members of the event-set; what I might call *supersession* (when the story takes a new turn, some new supposition supersedes the supposition that has been in the reader's mind for the time being) as the operative relation among members of the supposition-set; and the relation of *proponing* as that which holds between the events in the narrative set, and the suppositions as to outcome which they induce. These three relations satisfy the mathematical conditions insofar as: (1) no single event in a narrative propones more suppositions than one (open to question perhaps, but true on the whole); (2) if event e_2 succeeds event e_1 in the narrative series, then any supposition e_2 propones must supersede any supposition e_1 propones; and (3) if one event is not subsequent to another, the supposition it propones cannot supersede the supposition the other propones. To pursue the train of thought, it is necessary to be able to say that every event in a narrative propones *some* supposition as to outcome. This, however, seems reasonable along either of two lines. Either we may say that *what defines* a new member in the series of events, as against mere elaboration and detailing of an event, is that a new supposition as to outcome enters the reader's mind; or if we define 'event' otherwise, we may take it as an axiom that an event which in itself seems to propone no supposition, technically continues to propone the last supposition to come into play. I say 'technically', but there is surely no need: the idea seems to fit with our real experience of narrative reading. I said that there might 'to some extent' be a structure in the mathematical sense because certain points already seem to raise difficulty. For example, 'succession' is a transitive relation between events in a narrative, but if a second supposition supersedes a first one and then is superseded by a third, it is not easy to say that the third supersedes the first, since it might simply revert to it, and indeed this was precisely the situation with the Boccaccio narratives. The morphism could perhaps be preserved by adopting a modular arithmetic (to base 2 for the supposition sets in these tales): but I shall not pursue this point. The relation of superseding, of course, must not be thought to mean that one idea as to outcome now simply fills the reader's mind, which closes to the idea that filled it before. All will be aware of how the reading process, and so the idea of supposition itself, is more subtle, sophisticated, and contingent than that. The point was clarified at an early stage in the present chapter.

VI

The reader of this essay may by now have formed the thought that the analysis has limited interest because, after all, Boccaccio's tales themselves have limited interest. I willingly concede that the latter, at least, is true; and it is clear, indeed, from the fact that the set of suppositions as to outcome proponed by each narrative has two members only. Is there any likelihood that the categories of *event-set, proponing*, and *supposition-set* can offer substantial enlightenment in the case of a narrative intricate enough in its organization, and profound enough in its interests, to engage the modern reader's fullest attention?

I shall conclude the present discussion by approaching this question through an extremely, a temerariously brief review of certain aspects of Dostoevsky's *Crime and Punishment*. This encyclopaedic narrative with all its inexhaustible proliferations is surely a polar opposite from Boccaccio's witty tales of a few pages in length. Yet, as one reads the closing pages of Dostoevsky's immense book (of the main narrative, that is, for the epilogue

does not enter the present discussion) one has a strong sense that it
has a concern not only with the widest range of social life, character, conversation, or moral issues, but also with some quite
sharply definable matter of plot. It seems as if the narrative has to
reach a certain situation and, once it has reached it, that there will
be absolutely nothing more for it to do. Below the wealth and
variety one senses, all the time, some constant and powerful
narrative thrust ever at work.

The fact is (doubtless all are aware of it) that *Crime and Punishment* is not about crime and conviction, in the twentieth-century
thriller sense. It is about evil, and redemption or self-redemption
from evil; and at the level of plot this requires that Raskolnikov
should confess his crime while still free, doing so because Sonia
has called on him to confess, and because he understands and
accepts her call, and acts for her reasons alone. Only if this is the
resolution of the narrative does it embody what Dostoevsky has
to say in this novel about the issues of life.

The possibility of confession is there from early on: that is to
say, certain events propone it, from early on, as a supposition as to
outcome. But other possibilities as to outcome keep emerging
also. In Part 2 chapter 1 it seems that Raskolnikov must compromise himself irremediably during his first attendance at the
police station. In 2.6 he in fact confesses to Zamyotov in the
tavern – but it turns into a mock confession. In 3.6 it seems as if
Raskolnikov will be delivered up by Nikolai the workman (but so
far from that, in 4.5 Nikolai provides Raskolnikov with a fresh
chance for evasion by his own false confession). In 4.3
Razumukhin seems to guess that Raskolnikov is the murderer,
and in 4.4 Svidrigaylov, with his ear to the door, actually hears
him admit it to Sonia. Here are fresh possibilities that evidence
will be given against Raskolnikov before he can confess of his
own free will and on Sonia's terms. In 5.4, Raskolnikov's effective
confession to Sonia, we encounter also the suggestions that he
may commit suicide; that he may be mad; and that even if he
confesses the police will take it for a false confession. In the end he
takes the cross that Sonia offers him (I am referring to the incident
in literal terms, of course), but only after he has first declined it. In
6.2, Porfiry the police official advises Raskolnikov to confess and
says it will lessen his sentence: but that outcome would destroy
the novel's integrity – Raskolnikov, when he acts, must do so
only for Sonia's reason ('accept suffering and be redeemed by it –

that's what you must do': 5.4). Raskolnikov raises the possibility that he should 'run away', and in 6.5, Svidrigaylov makes this easy for him ('You'd better go off to America at once . . . I'll pay your fare'). At the very end, when Raskolnikov has obeyed Sonia and gone to the police station to confess, he learns that Svidrigaylov (the only one who could give him away) is dead. Hurriedly, he leaves. Redemptive confession as outcome suddenly recedes again; until on reaching the street he sees Sonia, waiting there to help until the very last. It is only then that he goes back and confesses. At once the narrative terminates.

That is no more than a sketch of the multitudinous divagations of the book, its endless renewing of the possibility that Sonia's words will in the event be wasted by suicide, madness, concealment, emigration – or confession that lacks the redemption of confession. What, however, in fact are these divagations? In the terminology of the present discussion, they are simply the *suppositions proposed* for the reader by the items in the event-set (or the successive event-sets, rather). The situation with regard to them is wholly different from the *Decameron* situation. There is not exciting simplicity of binary movement (a Barthesian *jouissance*, doubtless) but rather the progressive elimination of one supposition after another until it seems that *every possible* one has been brought forward and then rejected. Nor, of course, is this of interest only at the level of suspense and thrill. The point is that exactly this is what Dostoevsky wants his novel to say. Rack one's brains as one may, *nothing whatever* is any solution save only, and precisely, Sonia's solution. That is his first point. Second – I am less sure of this, but I believe it to be part of the story – whatever the multitudinous divagations of life may be, they will never be such as really to preclude or forestall such a redemptive solution and make it beyond the reach of man.

These two ideas could doubtless form part of the overt and explicit content of the narrative, and in an English mid-Victorian *Crime and Punishment* they might well have done so heavy-handedly. But Dostoevsky provided for them with a magisterial finality, by providing for them through structure alone. The first part of what he wanted to say is provided for by a constraint on the supposition set: that every possible supposition as to outcome must sooner or later in the narrative appear as an element in the supposition set, and moreover that every possible supposition save one (the one indicated in Sonia's words) must both appear and be superseded. The second part of it is provided for by a constraint on the series of events in the narrative: the number of events must be very large, but if there is any event which would be incompatible with what I will briefly call 'Sonia's outcome', it must not be a member of the event-set. This, I may note briefly, is why the character of Porfiry required such extraordinary, such virtuoso development. A police officer who must sense Raskolnikov's guilt, must call on him to confess, must do so in terms wholly other than Sonia's, must be willing to leave him time for all the other possibilities in fact to be rehearsed, and must be of a character such as in no way to detract from the full difficulty of Raskolnikov's position – that is an inadequate account of what was required: even Dostoevsky's inventive fertility must have been taxed by the problem he had set himself.

Those two constraints are purely formal constraints. They could be stated in symbolism, and they relate only to structure. Structure is what embodies and expresses the deepest and most central idea of the book, and I think that that is brought out through considering it with the help of the model developed here. If so, the situation is that a model developed for minor cases can clarify and even illuminate a major one.

2

Effectively complete enumeration in 'Phèdre'

There is a sense in which little happens in *Phèdre*, at least until shortly before the close of the play. It seems a strange thing to say of a momentous, passionate and absorbing drama, but the sense in which that is true is the sense of the expression 'what happens' that is relevant and dominant for much literature, perhaps for most *fictions*. In Act III scene iv, Thésée returns from abroad; in IV. ii he banishes Hippolyte, who suffers death only just outside the gates of Trézène (as is reported in v.vi); the death of Phèdre's *confidante* is reported in v.v; and Phèdre herself dies on stage in the closing lines of the play. So much for 'what happens' in the plain sense. Yet a drama like Phèdre is surely 'telling a story', and the story it tells is not one that begins more than half-way through and comprises those five events. What then *is* the 'what happens' in *Phèdre*?

It seems reasonable to look for the 'what happens' of this fiction, as of any other, among the matters that call out our interest or excitement, our sense that the work has moved on, our curiosity to know what the next phase of its moving on will be, or what its resolution will be, in view of the fact that the last phase was what it was. It is no original suggestion that these matters are, collectively, concerned with the consciousness and emotional lives of the four principal *dramatis personae:* Phèdre, Hippolyte, Aricie, Thésée.

The emotional lives of these characters are based comprehensively upon *what they believe about each other*. There is no need to argue at length that changes in the characters' beliefs about each other are something like the nerve of the action or 'narration' of the work. It will be toward these beliefs that the present analysis is directed: and towards the beliefs rather than the emotions and passions, for the reason that the former may be said to determine the latter as those do not determine the former. Also, it is much easier to establish a simple binary relation (viz., belief/disbelief) between a character and a belief than between a character and an emotion or passion. This remains true even though it is not always self-evident; and it remains true that one or two crucial changes of belief, in this particular work, *Phèdre*, spread over passages of dubiety or uncertainty, or simply absence from the stage, in such a way as prevents one from identifying exactly when the change occurs.

With those provisos, one can identify a quite small set of beliefs which are those at issue. The crucial set is considerably smaller than the total of beliefs which emerge into view at some point or other in the play. For example, in I.i, Théramène assumes that Hippolyte feels enmity towards Aricie; in I.iii, Oenone assumes that Phèdre feels enmity for Hippolyte, and Hippolyte feels the same for her. Phèdre assumes this of Hippolyte early in II.iii. Such beliefs are not, however, operative in the play as certain others are. What they contribute might perhaps be said to be an underlining of the surprise, and dramatic effect, latent in a character's changing his or her opinion about one of the crucial items of belief in the play.

What are these crucial items? They appear to be five in number, and the characters' successive relations to them of belief or disbelief makes up the substance of the play. I list them as follows:

A Phèdre loves Hippolyte
B Hippolyte loves Aricie
C Aricie loves Hippolyte
D Hippolyte does not love Phèdre
E Thésée is alive

It is a simplification to express the members of the key belief set in these or doubtless any other terms. The use of the word 'love' throughout the set A–E above, for example, is a substantial simplification. But the exact meaning which the word may bear from character to character is not at present germane. The argument nowhere assumes that the meaning is the same in any two cases. The word 'love' avoids irrelevant discussions rather than prejudges them.

The interest of a formal analysis of the set of beliefs held by each of the characters, as that set changes over the course of the play, is suggested by the number, and also by the dramatic prominence and power, of such changes – the degree to which the characters' acquiring, or discarding, their convictions about each other is what creates the substance and emotional life of the drama. The point is not only that characters hold these convictions intensely and that it is their convictions that induce their passions: but that relatively little else occurs in the play save these beliefs and their continual changing. The characters' lives are made up of a continual passage from one all-absorbing conviction to another. As the play proceeds, the sense grows that the author must almost be pressing this mode of construction to the limit: that there barely *could* be a greater number of spectacular cases of anagnorisis (which are also cases of peripeteia?) than actually occurs. Would any further permutations of belief, whether true or false, even have been possible? – this is what the reader or spectator feels inclined to wonder, as he reaches the closing scenes.

If that question is taken at face value, the answer in principle is that very many more would indeed be possible. It was suggested above that in pursuing this matter a number of the propositions which characters in the play believe or disbelieve (such, for instance, as that Hippolyte is actively hostile to Phèdre) might be disregarded, and only a key set of five propositions (A–E above) be considered. But those five propositions all enter, at some stage or another, into the mental life of each of the four principal characters. In principle, any of the four characters could either believe, or disbelieve, each of the five beliefs: and certainly each of the five beliefs is both believed, and disbelieved, by one or other of the major characters at some point in the play. In formal terms, each of the five items could take either of two values (believed, not believed). The number of possible sets of two items taken five at a time is $2^5 = 32$. Clearly, though, the characters do not each change their minds thirty-one times over. This way of approaching the structure of the play begins to appear absurd.

We can write out the set of beliefs held by the major characters at any point in the play, indicating whether each member of the main set is believed (1) or not believed (0). When this is done, the results look quite different from the impression of constant, intense, impassioned changefulness which is so powerful a part of the reading experience or the theatrical experience of the play. How does the discrepancy arise between a literary impression of constant changefulness, and the real situation, which is that only a small proportion of the theoretically possible re-arrangements occur in fact?

The obvious explanation would be that certain *general constraints* operate throughout the drama, ruling out many of the theoretically possible arrangements in advance: and that these constraints are so much part of the reader's experience or understanding, that he accepts them and their implications intuitively. They simply do not influence his reading or theatrical experience. Alternatively, we may say that if the belief arrangements (if I may so call them) which occur for each character throughout the play are scrutinized, the process ought to throw up something about two things: first, about the nature of these constraints; and second, about that dominant impression of almost unparalleled continuousness of re-arrangement as regards the characters' beliefs about each other. The two matters ought to stand out in some sort of relief at the same time.

The first constraint or limitation that may be suggested on the re-arrangement possibilities is an obvious one. It is that:

I. *No one can believe a false proposition about his own consciousness*

This is not put forward as a philosophical principle. As such it may or may not be true. What is meant is such possibilities as that Thésée might doubt his own existence, or that Phèdre might doubt that she feels passionately for Hippolyte: these seem to be excluded by the whole nature and *genre* of this play. No reader or spectator imagines for a moment that the development of the action may perhaps introduce such developments as these, and consequently no sense of limitation is created when it does not do so.

Perhaps, since these matters are not universally familiar, it might be worth while to set out the full possibilities of belief re-arrangement as a *matrix* which shows all thirty-two possible arrangements, and then to indicate which of these are as it were 'taken up' for each of the four principal characters.

Consider first the case of Hippolyte. By constraint I above, he cannot doubt either that he loves Aricie, or that he does not love Phèdre. Of the crucial items of the key belief-set, therefore, only three are available to his consciousness for re-arrangement. They are, A (Phèdre loves Hippolyte); C (Aricie loves Hippolyte); and E (Thésée is alive). At the start, he knows he loves Aricie, believes that Phèdre loves her husband, thinks Thésée is alive, and is ignorant of Aricie's love for himself. Setting the beliefs A to E out in columns, and using 'O' and 'I' as indicated, we may write this:

A	B	C	D	E	*Arrangement no.*
0	1	0	1	1	13

At the beginning of i.iv, there is a change. Panope says that it is useless for Phèdre to pray for the return of Thésée: 'Hippolyte son fils vient d'apprendre sa mort'. Hippolyte's position is now:

0	1	0	1	0	11

The next change comes in ii.iii, when he learns of Aricie's love for himself:

> J'accepte tous les dons que vous me voulez faire,
> Mais cet empire enfin si grand, si glorieux,
> N'est pas de vos présents le plus cher à mes yeux.

0	1	1	1	0	14

In ii.v, Hippolyte learns of Phèdre's love for himself. She says:

> Venge-toi, punis-moi d'un odieux amour:

which creates in him the new set of beliefs represented by

1	1	1	1	0	30

he now believes that Phèdre loves him and that Aricie loves him,

---

Figure 1. (*opposite*) The beliefs and belief-sets of characters in *Phèdre*. In *Phèdre*, there are five beliefs which, throughout the play, all the major characters either adopt, or reject (see p. 21). The left-hand half of this figure shows the thirty-two possible ways in which belief or disbelief in each of five items may be combined. '1' means believed and '0' means 'not believed'. The five beliefs are indicated by the capitals A to E.

The four columns in the right-hand half of the figure represent the four major characters in the drama. When any character, at *some point or other* in the drama, holds, jointly, all the five beliefs indicated on the left-hand side, a 'P' is inserted in the appropriate space in the column for that character. In respect of all the belief-sets that any given character never holds, the roman numerals indicate the 'constraint', as discussed in the text, that seems principally to eliminate that belief-set for that character.

Figure 1

Set no.	A	B	C	D	E	Hippolyte	Phèdre	Aricie	Thésée
1	0	0	0	0	0	I	II	I	I
	0	0	0	0	1	I	II	I	P
	0	0	0	1	0	I	III	I	I
	0	0	1	0	0	I	II	II	I
5	0	0	0	1	1	I	P	I	P
	0	0	1	1	0	I	III	P	I
	0	0	1	0	1	I	II	II	P
	0	0	1	1	1	I	V	III	V (VII)
9	0	1	0	0	0	I	II	I	I
	0	1	0	0	1	I	II	I	II
	0	1	0	1	0	P	III	I	I
	0	1	1	0	0	I	II	II	I
13	0	1	0	1	1	P	P	I	II (VII)
	0	1	1	1	0	P	III	P	I
	0	1	1	0	1	I	II	II	P
	0	1	1	1	1	III	VI	P	P
17	1	0	0	0	0	I	II	I	I
	1	0	0	0	1	I	II	I	II
	1	0	0	1	0	I	P	I	I
	1	0	1	0	0	I	II	II	I
21	1	0	0	1	1	I	III	I	VIII
	1	0	1	1	0	I	V	VII	I
	1	0	1	0	1	I	II	II	II
	1	0	1	1	1	I	III	VII	VIII
25	1	1	0	0	0	I	II	I	I
	1	1	0	0	1	I	II	I	II
	1	1	0	1	0	IV	III	I	I
	1	1	1	0	0	I	II	II	I
29	1	1	0	1	1	IV	P	I	VIII
	1	1	1	1	0	P	III	VI (or II)	I
	1	1	1	0	1	I	II	II	II
	1	1	1	1	1	P	P	P	P

and disbelieves that Thésée is alive. The only remaining re-arrangement is brought about, of course, by the return, and the physical presence, of Thésée in III.iv:

1   1   1   1   1   32

After this, Hippolyte is in full possession of the facts, and remains so (for this point, see p. 35 below).

For Hippolyte, therefore, only five re-arrangements occur out of a theoretical maximum of $2^5 = 32$. Completeness seems remote. But one must recall that in his case numbers 1 to 8 inclusive of the matrix, and also 17 to 24 inclusive, are ruled out because constraint I rules out all arrangements of the form $\cdot\ 0\ \cdot\cdot\cdot$ (since Hippolyte cannot *not* believe that he loves Aricie); and all arrangements of the form $\cdot\cdot\cdot\ 0\ \cdot$ are also ruled out by this same constraint (Hippolyte cannot believe that he loves Phèdre, he knows he does not). This excludes, additionally, everything of the form $\cdot\ 1\ \cdot\ 0\ \cdot$, i.e. 9, 10, 12, 15, 25, 26, 28, 31. There thus remains to consider only why arrangements 16, 27 and 29 do not occur. Does that fact suggest to us any further constraint which is reasonable intrinsically and would explain their absence?

What, if anything, excludes those arrangements? It is important to notice that here the discussion could proceed in either of two very different ways. We could argue, for example, that arrangements 27 and 29 both include the form $1\ \cdot\ 0\ \cdot\cdot$. That is to say, they require Hippolyte to learn of Phèdre's passion while he is still ignorant of Aricie's. We could then argue that this requires him to believe arrangement 27, or 29, prior to II.iii if at all (that is the scene in which he declares his love for Aricie). Following that, we could then argue that prior to this scene we do not see Hippolyte speaking to anyone who could have told him (he does not meet Phèdre, Théramène believes Phèdre to be at best indifferent to Hippolyte, Oenone knows of Phèdre's passion by the end of Act I but could not reveal it unless she had Phèdre's permission). Quite probably, arrangements 27 and 29 could *de facto* be excluded along these lines, and similarly with many of the belief-arrangements that other characters could in principle hold, but in fact do not hold.

This level of argument, however, is relatively weak: it depends for its validity on the details of organization of this play exactly as we have it – the exact sequence of scenes, the precise opinions of the minor characters. Had any of these details been differen organized by Racine, such arguments would at once lose all their effectiveness. Are there arguments of another and more powerful kind, such as might hold good, not simply of the play exactly as Racine wrote it, but of – for the moment I shall put this quite loosely – of any play whatever which (a) was based on the same primary belief-set (A to E, p. 21 above) and (b) was not somehow *fundamentally different in kind* from Racine's play? It is this kind of argument which will be pursued in what follows.

How might such a more general and more powerful argument run in the particular case of Hippolyte? I should like to interpolate here that in much of what follows I am not even looking for something like apodeictic certainty, but rather just for arguments enough to exclude reasonable doubt. This being said by way of preliminary, we may go on to say that – in brief – *any* belief-set of the form $1 \cdot 0 \cdot \cdot$ (any set, that is, indicating that Hippolyte knows of Phèdre's love before he knows of Aricie's), would set the author an insoluble problem. Why is this? Because if Hippolyte does not learn of Phèdre's love until after Thésée's return, he cannot present a suspicious appearance to Thésée at the moment of his return; and if he does not, Thésée's suspicions cannot be immediately aroused or confirmed on that account. Then Hippolyte must learn of the matter before Thésée's return. But what must Hippolyte do if he learns, in his father's absence, that his father's wife has an adulterous and incestuous love for him? I suggest (the point is developed below) that he must leave Trézène immediately. Then there can be no play remotely like the one we have, save for a single possible course. This is, that Hippolyte should learn about Phèdre $(1 \cdot \cdot \cdot \cdot)$; and should immediately seek out Aricie to take leave of her because of his consequent self-banishment; and that Thésée should return before he can leave in fact.

But this construction would be exposed to the difficulty already mentioned (that Hippolyte cannot be found in suspicious circumstances by Thésée at the moment of his return) and also to others. First, that under these circumstances Hippolyte cannot declare his love to Aricie, save under circumstances which make his motives open to suspicion. Second, that in this situation Aricie cannot implicitly believe, and perhaps even cannot learn at all, of Phèdre's guilty passion. No one can tell her but Hippolyte, and the more he is under suspicion the less can he tell her, and the less can she believe him if he does. But if she cannot learn of that guilty passion she cannot (see v.iv) be instrumental in the enlightenment of Thésée about the matter. But if she cannot be instrumental, there is no one who can be instrumental save Phèdre (the rules governing the rôles of minor characters exclude them all). When Phèdre confesses to her husband, it has to be the end of the play. Under these circumstances, Aricie would simply have no rôle at all.

We may conclude that arrangements 27 (1 1 0 1 0) and 29 (1 1 0 1 1) are excluded by general and fundamental considerations; it remains to identify the constraints which underlie and validate this argument. They seem to be the following. Why cannot Thésée's suspicions be aroused in the absence of evidence? Because, I suggest:

II. *Characters must form and hold the beliefs rational on the evidence before them*[1]

Why must Hippolyte leave Trézène at once if he learns of Phèdre's passion, and why must he declare his love for Aricie while he is still ignorant of that passion? Because:

III. *The actions and motives of characters must at all times be comprehensible and unambiguous*

Why cannot Aricie simply not learn of Hippolyte's love for her, not tell him of hers for him, and not play any part in the enlightenment of Thésée? Because:

IV. *Every character must have a rôle of some kind*

What of arrangement 16 (0 1 1 1 1)? This requires that Hippolyte should not learn of Phèdre's passion until after Thésée's return. But to construct the play like this is again to create insoluble problems. In these circumstances, Hippolyte's behaviour on Thésée's return cannot be such as to arouse Thésée's suspicions. How then can Thésée form those suspicions? Oenone cannot tell him (as she does in the play we have) because she can do so only to save her mistress from betrayal, and if Hippolyte does not know the guilty secret, he has nothing to betray. Phèdre cannot do so herself by constraint III: she can have no comprehensible motive for causing the destruction of the man she loves when

---

1. I take this to mean two things: (a) characters must no form irrational beliefs, given the evidence; (b) characters must abandon beliefs that fresh evidence renders irrational.

he can do her no harm. Arrangement 16 also is therefore excluded; and since no other possibilities remain, the series:

```
0    1    0    1    1
0    1    0    1    0
0    1    1    1    0
1    1    1    1    0
1    1    1    1    1
```

i.e., arrangements 13, 10, 14, 30 and 32, those which we found in fact to occur, may be termed – the expression will be used again later – an *effectively complete enumeration*.

Phèdre's case presents certain special difficulties. First, there seems to be an interval during which Phèdre's infatuation with Hippolyte actually ceases. She learns of Thésée's return in III.iii (Oenone says: 'Le roi, qu'on a cru mort, va parôitre en ces lieux') and almost immediately, speaking of Hippolyte, tells her confidante 'Je le vois comme un monstre effroyable à mes yeux'. As soon however as she learns that Hippolyte loves Aricie, her own passion for him is re-animated:

> Quel feu mal étouffé dans mon coeur se réveille (IV.v)

It would be possible (that very 'mal étouffé' invites it, indeed) to claim as the proper account of the matter that she never ceases to 'love' Hippolyte; and that we have here the exceptional case where constraint I ceases to hold.

Thus Phèdre is not committed even to the form $1 \cdot \cdot \cdot \cdot$ throughout the play. *Prima facie*, all five members of the general belief-set are available to Phèdre to believe or disbelieve in the course of the play: in principle the number of re-arrangements of five beliefs each of which may be either accepted or rejected is $2^5 = 32$, which is doubtless far beyond anything practicable in a literary work.

What happens in fact? Phèdre's first clear position as regards her beliefs come in I.iv, when Panope's announcement obliges her (by constraint II) to believe in her husband's death:

A	B	C	D	E	*Arrangement no.*
1	0	0	1	0	19

In III.iii she learns that Thésée is alive, thereby and simultaneously ceases to feel a passionate attachment to Hippolyte, and (by constraint I) immediately becomes aware of that. We may write this:

$$0 \quad 0 \quad 0 \quad 1 \quad 1 \qquad\qquad 5$$

In IV.v, Phèdre learns that Hippolyte loves Aricie. The consequences are first, her own passion for Hippolyte re-awakens and (by constraint I) she at once knows this. We may therefore write

$$0 \quad 1 \quad 0 \quad 1 \quad 1 \qquad\qquad 13$$

and then

$$1 \quad 1 \quad 0 \quad 1 \quad 1 \qquad\qquad 29$$

Almost immediately also, Phèdre infers that Aricie loves Hippolyte. Racine in fact builds this into Phèdre's language at once, powerfully but inconspicuously. When she tells Oenone of her discovery about Hippolyte, even at the first Aricie's love for him is part of what she has to say (IV,vi)

> Aricie à trouvé le chemin de son coeur . . .
> Ils aiment. . . .

This requires further discussion, but we may write:

$$1 \quad 1 \quad 1 \quad 1 \quad 1 \qquad\qquad 32$$

Phèdre's case may be more complicated than Hippolyte's; but certain substantial sub-sets of the whole set of belief-arrangements may be excluded in respect of her forthwith. First, by constraint II and (as it applies at all times to the conduct not of herself but of Hippolyte) constraint III, all arrangements of the form $\cdots 0 \cdot$ are self-exclusive. Phèdre cannot at any time form the belief that Hippolyte returns her passion. This excludes no fewer than sixteen theoretically possible arrangements, viz. 1, 2, 4, 7, 9, 10, 12, 15, 17, 18, 20, 23, 25, 26, 28, 31.

Also, Phèdre can only change her attitude to belief A if she ceases to love Hippolyte or if, having done so, she then begins to love him again. What circumstances could bring this about? In fact, she ceases to love Hippolyte on the shock of Thésée's return (together with the knowledge that Hippolyte knows of her guilty passion) and her love is re-awakened when she learns that Hippolyte is capable of love. Could any other event bring these changes about? Not, I think, unless constraint III be abandoned in respect of Phèdre. Otherwise we may say that all arrangements of the form $0 \cdots 0$ (Phèdre ceases to love Hippolyte while she still

thinks Thésée is dead) and 1 0 · · 1 (Phèdre begins to love Hippolyte again, after Thésée's return but without her knowing of
Hippolyte's susceptibility to Aricie) are excluded. This excludes
arrangements 1, 3, 4, 6, 9, 10, 11, 14; and also 18, 21, 23, 24 (some
of these were of course excluded – see above – already). Arrangements 8, 16, 22, 27 and 30 remain to be considered.

Of these, arrangements 8 and 22 imply that Phèdre learns that
Aricie loves Hippolyte before she learns that Hippolyte loves
Aricie. This, I suggest, is eliminable by a further constraint:

V. *Events which would make a work digressive and would
   diminish its tension do not occur*
   Unless · 1 · · · , the arrangement · · 1 · · can have no
interest for Phèdre or anyone else (save of course Aricie). Further,
16 (0 1 1 1 1) is excluded *ex hypothesi* because what it means is that
the one event which could re-kindle Phèdre's passion (finding out
that Hippolyte is himself capable of passion) does not re-kindle it.
Therefore nothing can re-kindle it. But this makes any dénouement impossible and:

VI. *Events which make a dénouement impossible do not occur*
    Arrangements 27 (1 1 0 1 0) and 30 (1 1 1 1 0) both imply
(by · 1 · · 0) that Phèdre learns of Hippolyte's love for Aricie
before Thésée's return. But then constraint III will prevent her
from telling Hippolyte of her own passion for him (or allowing
Oenone, as would correspond to Euripides' play, to do so). In that
case, Thésée's suspicions will not be aroused, etc., and so 27 and
30 are excluded; and once again there is an *effectively complete
enumeration*, in that every theoretically possible arrangement
either occurs in the play or is excluded by the constraints. The full
situation with regard to these constraints will be discussed below.

Aricie's case is simpler than Phèdre's. By constraint I she can
adopt no belief-arrangement of the form · · 0 · · , because if she
loves Hippolyte she must know she loves Hippolyte. Constraint
II makes it impossible for her to adopt any arrangement of the
form · · · 0 · , given constraint III. If Hippolyte, that is to say, is
precluded by constraint III from behaving ambiguously, Aricie
cannot believe that the man she loves would behave ambiguously
– still less, that he would form an adulterous and incestuous
passion. If Aricie can adopt no belief-arrangement which has the

form · · 0 · · . arrangements 1, 2, 3, 5, 9, 10, 11, 13, 17, 18, 19, 21, 25, 26, 27 and 29 are excluded; if none of the form · · · 0 · , the further exclusions will be 4, 7, 12, 15, 20, 23, 28 and 31. Aricie in fact adopts, successively, the following belief-arrangements. After II.i. (Ismène: 'Thésée est mort, madame, et vous seul en doutez') her position is:

A	B	C	D	E		*Arrangement no.*
0	0	1	1	0		6

in II.ii, after Hippolyte's declaration, it is:

0	1	1	1	0		14

In one way, the sequence of events thereafter is uncertain. By v.i, when Aricie says to Hippolyte, 'Quoi! vous pouvez vous taire en ce péril extrême?', Aricie clearly knows both of Phèdre's passion, and of Thésée's return (she knows of his anger). But it is not perfectly clear which she learns about first – whether, that is, Hippolyte tells her about Phèdre (as was argued above, no one else can) before Thésée's return, or after. Presumably, however, we must think that he tells her about it after Thésée's return; and that he does so only as part of explaining the truth of the circumstances which have placed him in a false light and led to his banishment. If so, we have the further arrangements

0	1	1	1	1		16

and then, at some point between the end of IV.ii, and the opening line (quoted above) of v.i, – doubtless we are meant to think it comes almost immediately prior to that line – the arrangement:

1	1	1	1	1		32

Arrangements 8, 22, 24, and 30 remain unaccounted for: what, if anything, precludes their appearance in the play?

Arrangements 22 and 24 both contain the form 1 0 · · · . For Aricie they indicate, most obviously, that she learns of Phèdre's passion before Hippolyte declares his love for herself. This is impossible, because by constraint III neither Phèdre nor Oenone could tell Aricie (the act would be absurd), and by the same constraint Hippolyte could do so only under the extreme circumstances mentioned above. The alternative possibility is that Aricie should cease to believe in Hippolyte's love; but I propose that this be excluded by a further constraint:

VII. *Conversions from false beliefs to true are irreversible*

It may be noted in passing that every change of belief in the play, for every character, does in fact conform to this. Arrangements 22 and 24 are thus excluded. Arrangements 8 and 30 cannot appear for other reasons. Arrangement 8 implies that Aricie learns of Hippolyte's love only after Thésée's return. But if that happens, either Hippolyte must tell her (for no one else can) when he is already suspected of an adulterous and incestuous passion (which is contrary to constraint III), or, Thésée must form his suspicions about Hippolyte substantially later than the moment of his homecoming. This in turn implies either that he disregards the suspicious circumstances attending that; or, that it is not attended by suspicious circumstances; or finally, that his suspicions are aroused by a decisive act like Phèdre's suicide and dying confession (as in Euripides). But constraint III makes it impossible for Phèdre to confess 'substantially later' than Thésée's homecoming, for the wife whose motives are unambiguous could only do so at once or not at all; and constraint II precludes the possibilities both that Thésée does not modify his beliefs when he encounters the suspicious-looking reception, and that he does modify them when he has no ground for doing so. Arrangement 8 (0 0 1 1 1) is therefore excluded.

Arrangement 30 implies that Aricie learns of Hippolyte's love for her, *and also of Phèdre's passion for him*, prior to Thésée's return. This seems to be precluded by constraint III (Hippolyte would hardly have any adequate ground for telling her, so how could she know?), but more by constraint VI. If Aricie knew of Phèdre's passion she would be obliged to tell Hippolyte (assuming, *par impossible*, that it was not he who had told her) and be willing to flee from Trézène with him. That eventuality is precluded by constraint VI, unless Thésée returned just as they were in the act of leaving. But then, more than ever, constraint II would preclude Thésée's becoming suspicious. Arrangement 30 thus appears to be not a real possibility, and in respect of Aricie also, we may say that there is an *effectively complete enumeration*.

Thésée cannot doubt belief E at any point (constraint I). Arrangements 1, 3, 4, 6, 9, 11, 12, 14, 17, 19, 20, 22, 25, 27, 28 and 30 therefore cannot arise. At the moment of his return he of course adopts the arrangement:

A   B   C   D   E   *Arrangement no.*
0   0   0   1   1   5

In iv.i, he is incredulously persuaded by Oenone to adopt

0   0   0   0   1   2

In v.iii, when he is alone with Aricie, he becomes persuaded (more or less indifferently, one may note in passing) of her love for Hippolyte:

0   0   1   0   1   7

To decide when Thésée next changes his mind is not particularly easy, but presumably he becomes convinced that Aricie's love was genuinely returned as he listens to Théramène's account of her meeting with Hippolyte at the moment of Hippolyte's death:

0   1   1   0   1   15

but by constraint II, this must lead him immediately to:

0   1   1   1   1   16

which is his position at the beginning of v.i (when he refers to his 'cruel soupçon'); and by the end of the scene, of course, his position is:

1   1   1   1   1   32

That still leaves ten theoretically possible belief-arrangements for Thésée, other than those actually appearing or already excluded. But certain further exclusions are self-evident. If Thésée believes that Hippolyte loves Aricie he cannot (by constraint II) believe that he also has a guilty passion for his stepmother. This precludes all arrangements of the form · 1 · 0 · , that is to say (ignoring arrangements already precluded) 10, 26 and 31. Similarly, Thésée cannot (also by constraint II) believe that Phèdre has a guilty passion for Hippolyte, and also that he has a guilty passion for her. This is because only Oenone (iii.iii 'Fais ce que tu voudras . . .' Phèdre says to her in iii.iii), or Phèdre herself, could tell him of such guilty passions (one a falsehood, the other not), and insofar as he believed that Phèdre had such a guilty passion, neither she nor her confidante would be a reliable witness; and so, by constraint II, Thésée's believing what they said would be precluded. This precludes all arrangements, then, of the form 1 · · 0 · : that is, it further precludes arrangements 18 and 23. There remain arrangements 8, 13, 21, 24 and 29.

Arrangements 21 (1 0 0 1 1), 24 (1 0 1 1 1) and 29 (1 1 0 1 1) all presuppose that Thésée learns of his wife's guilty passion before he learns (either at all, as in 21, or fully, as in 24 and 29) of the love between Hippolyte and Aricie. But this is precluded by constraint V, unless we assume that the play can end without Thésée's learning these facts at all. This, I suggest, would be contrary to the further constraint:

VIII. *All the characters must reach a final state of full knowledge*
        Only arrangements 8 (0 0 1 1 1) and 13 (0 1 0 1 1) remain to be considered. These two (as has so often been the case, throughout the discussion, with a group of arrangements that have come up for discussion together) have something substantial in common, if we consider them not just formally but as genuine accounts of the condition of Thésée's mind. They represent the two possible variations on the situation where Thésée has learnt something of the love between Hippolyte and Aricie, though not the whole truth about it, while he has no suspicion of Hippolyte's involvement with Phèdre. If he has no suspicions it can only be because *either* he has not yet formed any suspicions, *or* because he has abandoned them (this would not, of course, be inconsistent with constraint VII). Here again, it is important to distinguish, as was done on pp. 26–7, between arguments conclusive for this play of Racine's as we have it in detail, and arguments generally conclusive. After the circumstances of his reception in III.iv, constraint II means that Thésée cannot not form suspicions, or abandon suspicions that he has once formed, save by coming to believe in Phèdre's guilt, which must end the play. But more generally: given that Thésée believes · 1 · · · as in 13 (Hippolyte loves Aricie), constraint II requires that he does not believe · · · 0 · (Hippolyte is guilty as regards Phèdre), unless Thésée ceases to believe that Hippolyte loves Aricie. But that would contravene constraint VII. On the other hand, for Thésée to learn that Aricie loves an Hippolyte whom he believes to be quite innocent of guilty passion contravenes constraint V, unless it is the preliminary to his learning that her love is reciprocated. But if Thésée once believes · 1 1 1 1 he cannot come to believe · · · 0 1: to do so would contravene constraint VII. Arrangements 8 and 13, we may infer, are thus both precluded. But they were the only arrangements left, other than those actually occurring. Once again, there is therefore an *effectively complete enumeration*.

The upshot of the discussion is therefore that, given the set of constraints which have emerged in the course of it, Racine has, for each of his major characters, achieved a complete enumeration of all the genuinely available belief-sets. It really seems as if no play could have been written which introduced arrangements additional to those Racine introduces, unless the author had abandoned one or more of the constraints which Racine observed; or, of course, had not started with the characters, or operated with the belief-set, which he did start and operate with. It is of course possible to imagine plays on the general subject of this myth in which a self-deluding Phèdre thought she was remaining constant to Thésée but really was consumed by a passion for Hippolyte; or one in which a schizophrenic Hippolyte refuses to believe the officially validated news of his father's death; or one in which Hippolyte was meant to love Aricie although he also assaulted his step-mother; or one in which Phèdre died before she ever discovered Hippolyte's love for Aricie; or, of course, one in which there is no Aricie at all, as in Euripides. These possibilities involve, respectively, the suspension of constraints I, II, III, and VIII; and the supposition that there is no Aricie would suspend one item in the basic belief-set A to E.

It is now time to resume, and examine, the set of constraints which have emerged in the course of the discussion; and it will be obvious enough that they are not a definitive or fundamental set at all:

    I. No one can believe a false proposition about his own consciousness
    II. Characters must form and hold the beliefs rational on the evidence before them
    III. The actions and motives of characters must at all times be comprehensible and unambiguous
    IV. Every character must have a rôle of some kind
    V. Events which would make a work digressive and would diminish its tension do not occur
    VI. Events which make a dénouement impossible do not occur
    VII. Conversions from false beliefs to true are irreversible
    VIII. All the characters must reach a final state of full knowledge

These eight constraints emerged in the course of the discussion, simply as what would make it possible to claim effectively complete enumerations. They are doubtless part of a larger whole of general conventions (part social, part psychological, part literary,

or any combination of these, maybe) within which the play
Phèdre, as doubtless other works, came to be written. The
catalogue of constraints listed above may perhaps be re-ordered
to some extent: perhaps constraint II, for example, could be held
to include constraint I, and constraint IV could be taken as a
special case of constraint V. If this were agreed, we would then
have constraints II and III, requiring that characters should behave
orderly and rationally, and this could be seen as flowing from the
familiar dramatic convention of *vraisemblance*. Then we should
have constraints V–VIII, which look like *genre* conventions
calling for a work to be in some sense progressive, non-digressive
and climatic or 'culminative'. There is no reason to suppose that
this particular discussion has elicited the full conception of what
such a work might be like or what requirements such a conception might impose upon works that conformed to it; but this
conception of a certain kind of literary work seems part of what is
operative in our minds when, seeing or reading Phèdre, we have
that intuition of incessant, unremitting re-arrangement of the
dramatic situation which has here been analysed as *effectively
complete enumeration*.

3

Narrative process in 'Middlemarch'

The subject of continuity and discontinuity in fiction has not, I think, been much discussed. There is a sense in which it is a somewhat pedestrian subject. But not altogether so. Needless to say, there are novels (especially twentieth-century ones, though by no means those exclusively) which depend for their total effect upon creating what might be called relative discontinuities – although a complete discontinuity and unrelatedness between one part of any single work and another part must be a contradiction in terms. Most of the major novels of the nineteenth century seem to show a high degree of continuity from beginning through to end: though it seems also that there are several kinds of continuity, and indeed that there are both kinds of it, and sub-kinds. This discussion will try to identify some of these as they appear in *Middlemarch*, and what is meant by 'continuity' will I hope emerge.

One might begin by thinking loosely of a discontinuity as a strikingly 'fresh start' in the narrative. Such a fresh start might occur in any book in the middle of a chapter; but the more natural place to expect it would be at the end of a chapter, or book, or even 'Volume' of the narrative as a whole. 'Prelude' and 'Finale' aside, *Middlemarch* has eighty-six chapters. Only five, out of that large number, dispose the reader to say that the chapter makes a fresh start, after a complete break with what has gone before. This does not of course mean with everything that has gone before: that would mean there was no single novel. It means, with what has gone immediately before – with the closing page or so of the preceding chapter. That is what is meant by proximate 'continuity': and such a degree of proximate continuity is a surprising and surely remarkable thing.

The five isolated exceptions are chapters 15, 19, 23, 28, and 40;

and in these five cases there are special considerations. Chapter 19 opens with a general historical intimation of the year in which the narrative is set ('When George the Fourth was still reigning over the privacies of Windsor, when the Duke of Wellington was Prime Minister, when Mr Vincy was mayor of the old corporation of Middlemarch . . .') and then focusses this upon the events of the novel by the words 'Mrs Casaubon, born Dorothea Brooke, had taken her wedding journey to Rome'. This proximate *dis*continuity is perhaps explained and justified in that it marks the major shift of *locale* from Middlemarch to Rome. The discontinuity between chapters 27 and 28 may be seen as counterpart to that, marking the return from Rome to Middlemarch. The discontinuity between chapters 14 and 15 (the latter of which opens with the digression on Fielding's digressiveness) marks the interruption of the novel's onward flow in order to move back into the past and provide the reader with the facts of Lydgate's earlier life – with, in other words, a uniquely 'interrupting' and discontinuous chapter.

Two chapters only out of eighty-six, therefore, show this proximate discontinuity, while at the same time they continue the main account of Middlemarch events. Chapter 40 opens with an explicit theoretical justification of why it does so: 'In watching effects, if only of an electric battery, it is often necessary to change our place and examine a particular mixture or group at some distance . . . The group I am moving towards is Caleb Garth's breakfast-table'. An electric battery, I suppose, involves remote effects in that it can dis-charge, or discharge and be re-charged from outside: in chapter 40 the depleted and discharged battery of Mr Brooke's credit as landlord is re-charged by the proposal to appoint Caleb as agent; and Caleb's domestic economy, one might say, is re-charged by the current from Brooke's wealth. The only chapter in the whole book where there is a proximate discontinuity that has, as it were, nothing to justify it in some special way is 23, which (one may note) opens book III, and also volume II, of the novel with the words 'Fred Vincy, *as we have seen*, had a debt on his mind'. The one chapter, that is, which seems simply to reject the canons of continuity general in the book, even so includes in its opening words an explicit invitation to recognize some continuity that is other than the proximate kind.

It remains to demonstrate what up to now I have merely asserted – the prevalence of proximate continuity throughout –

and to identify the processes which achieve that. Once it is fully recognized, the sustained care and the marked dexterity and ingenuity underlying that will strike one as remarkable. Established critical approaches do not bring this out or indeed cause one to expect it, and when its full extent is seen it leaves a strong impression in the mind. 'I had no idea George Eliot would be at such pains for a thing like that', we incline to say. On the other hand the processes involved are not obscure. The most obvious and also commonest is simply when some given chapter continues the dialogue, or action, between the same characters as the previous one: this is a continuity between chapters of the same kind as what so often maintains continuity page by page, even line by line. In chapter 1, Dorothea and Celia converse; in 2, the family is at dinner, and once again Dorothea is present, but engaged now in a dialogue that includes her uncle Mr Brooke and the guests Sir James and Casaubon (Celia, we soon find, is there too). In 3, there is a jump forward in time, but Brooke and Casaubon converse together once again, while Dorothea and then Sir James soon enter the narrative too. Chapter 4 opens with a conversation between Dorothea and, once more, Celia. Chapter 5 involves Dorothea, Casaubon and Celia again. There are perhaps a half-dozen extended blocks of narrative of this kind in all; the general point need not be laboured.

More interesting is the way in which proximate continuitites, sometimes extended over a considerable extent, can be achieved when the continuity is sustained, as it were, by being passed to and fro among otherwise widely disparate characters. This happens the more readily, for reasons that may suggest themselves, in the later stages of a novel. Thus chapter 42 depicts the domestic life of Casaubon and Dorothea; in 43, the same Dorothea calls on Rosamond when Will Ladislaw is there; in 44 she goes on to see Lydgate. Chapter 45 begins as a more general picture of Lydgate and various of his patients or those who observe him and his career, and takes him back to Rosamond at the end of a tiring day.

Another example: chapter 75 is between Rosamond and Lydgate, 76 between Lydgate and Dorothea, 77 between Dorothea, Will and Rosamond, 78 between Will and Rosamond, and later between Rosamond and Lydgate. Chapter 79 is a dialogue between Will and Lydgate after Rosamond has gone to bed.

Now for something a little less straightforward. I mentioned earlier that proximate continuity through *continuing dramatis per-*

sonae held, from chapter 1 through to 5. Between chapters 5 and 6 it hardly holds at all: chapter 6 opens with a conversation between Mrs Cadwallader and Mrs Fichett, and only Mr Brooke has a speaking part in both chapters (in ch. 5 this being early on and very brief). Another kind of continuity, however, is written into the text. Casaubon leaves the Brooke's house at the end of chapter 5, and chapter 6 opens:

> As Mr. Casaubon's carriage was passing out of the gateway, it *arrested the entrance* of a pony phaeton driven by a lady

everyone knows that this was Mrs Cadwallader, though Casaubon was far away and didn't even recognize her. Unmistakably, the Casaubon carriage appears in the text for the sole purpose of providing a continuity with chapter 5 that one might call *continuity by reference*. Casaubon is mentioned at the beginning of chapter 5 to link 5 to 4, where he has appeared. This form appears seldom enough, but another example is chapter 61. Chapter 60 closes with the night-time street scene when Raffles accosts Will Ladislaw. Chapter 61 opens with something quite different, a domestic scene in the Bulstrodes' house. But the first words are Mrs Bulstrode's 'Nicholas. . . . there has been such a disagreeable man here asking for you'. It was Raffles of course.

A striking example occurs between chapters 70 and 71. Chapter 70 closes with Lydgate's telling Farebrother of how Bulstrode has lent him the money; 71 opens with Bambridge, Hawley and others seeing Bulstrode as he rode past them while they stood gossiping in the street, and Bambridge then telling the story about Bulstrode that he picked up from Raffles in Bilkley. Apart from riding by in silence, Bulstrode plays no part in the action in chapter 71; the continuity is mainly provided by his being referred to in first the one scene, then the other.

Between, say, chapters 31 and 32, there seems to be a proximate continuity by reference and also something more. Chapter 31 closes with Lydgate's visit, as prospective son-in-law, to Mr Vincy. Vincy is full of the thought that Fred will soon inherit from the dying Featherstone. Chapter 32 resumes this reference to Fred, but by saying that the Mayor's confident hopes for Fred were 'a feeble emotion' by comparison with what was felt by the whole tribe of Featherstone's blood-relations (Jonah Waule, Martha Cranch, etc.). In other words, part of the continuity is a continuity from one potential legatee *to all the others*. We may compare how in chapter 36 Vincy laments his personal shortage of money in the then difficult times, and 37 opens by saying that his 'doubt' was 'a feeble *type* of the uncertainties in provincial opinion at that time'; which leads into something of a survey of political opinions and activities in Middlemarch generally. That is to say, here too the continuity of the novel is maintained by a process of something like *generalization*. Yet almost at once, this survey of Middlemarch politics and opinion is concentrated once again: on Ladislaw's editorship of the *Pioneer* and collaboration with Brooke. Chapter 16 opens with a dinner party at the Vincys' with many of the guests speaking generally to each other. But in the later stages of a dinner party, any two guests may seek each other out. '[Rosamond] and Lydgate readily got into conversation'. They are *selected* from the general, and the continuity comes from how they were present all the time, as it were stored up in readiness for this process of selection. One may compare chapter 73, in which Lydgate reflects alone about Bulstrode's position, and also Rosamond's, followed by 74, which opens: 'In Middlemarch a wife could not long remain ignorant that *the town* held a bad opinion of her husband'; then surveys the talk generally, through Mrs Hackbutt, Mrs Sprage, Mrs Toller and other such ladies; and in its closing pages selects out the individual conversations through which Mrs Bulstrode herself came to piece together the truth. Again, continuity is through generalization and specialization.

Thus four processes of proximate continuity may be distinguished: what might be called continuity of the *cast*, continuity by *reference* (this may be either forwards, or backwards, incidentally), and what I have been referring to by the words *generalization*, and *selection*. These latter processes are of exceptional importance in *Middlemarch*, where much of the purpose of the novel is to show systematically how the individualized biographies of the principal characters reflect, react upon, and are seen by, the general life of the town.

Perhaps these last two narrative processes may be set in a somewhat general light: it seems that once an author can set up a situation like a dinner party, where any character may be talking to any other one, then any process of selection and specialization may be adopted, from all those present to, say, any two of them, and proximate continuity will be maintained. Or again, wherever some event involving individuals is likely to interest a social group generally, or to be generally representative of it, proximate continuity can be preserved within a process of generalizing.

Before proceeding to processes of indirect continuity, I should like to examine proximate continuity within a particular chapter, 31, in some detail. Among other things, this will stress that discussion of continuity between chapters is part only of the matter of proximate continuity.

Chapter 31 seems to comprise no fewer than seven short episodes. They are: (a) a flirtatious conversation between Lydgate and Rosamond which begins 'Lydgate that evening spoke to Miss Vincy of Mrs. Casaubon' and is thereby given proximate continuity with the preceding chapter, at the close of which Dorothea both appears and is referred to; (b) an intricate bridge-passage to which I revert; (c) a conversation between Mrs Bulstrode and Mrs Plymdale; (d) a conversation between Mrs Bulstrode and Rosamond; (e) one between Mrs Bulstrode and Lydgate; (f) one between Lydgate and Farebrother (g) a very short report of a conversation between Lydgate and Mrs Vincy; (h) the decisive scene when Lydgate calls at the Vincys' house, finds Rosamond alone there, and becomes engaged to her.

Clearly there is proximate continuity by 'continuity of the cast', to and fro, in the action from (c) through to (h). But what continuity, if any, exists between (a) and (b), or (b) and (c)? At the end of (a) the narrative says in effect everyone in Middlemarch had an eye to Rosamond's doings' and then (quoting the text *verbatim*), 'Aunt Bulstrode, *for example*, came a little oftener . . . to see Rosamond. . .' What has happened is a condensed process of generalization, followed by the process of specialization, of free re-selection, which that makes possible. That concludes what I called episode (b). Episode (c) begins 'Now Mrs. Bulstrode had a long-standing intimacy with Mrs. Plymdale', and this means that proximate continuity between (b) and (c) is secured by reference in (b) forward to (c): one of the characters in (c), i.e. Mrs Bulstrode, is referred to in the bridge-passage of narrative which I have labelled (b). It is surely the case that the ingenuity of the devices for securing proximate continuity, and the constancy and density with which they appear, come rather as surprises.

It is time to move on to indirect continuity. Indirect continuity seems to be most substantially created by a familiar process which I shall call 'initiative and response'; and it is this process, I believe, which creates the decisive and massive continuities – not only, needless to say, in *Middlemarch* – and for which proximate continuities provide only something of an unobtrusively continuing substratum. Thus within chapter 5 the initiative of Casaubon's letter to Dorothea, proposing marriage, is continued in the response of Dorothea's accepting him. In chapter 6 Mrs Cadwallader tells Sir James this fact and adds that Celia likes him. We find continuity created by his response to this in chapter 8: 'he was beginning to pay small attentions to Celia'. It is also clear, of course, that something links chapters 5 and 6 in respect specifically of these matters, not just through the proximate continuity discussed earlier.

A much longer indirect continuity through initiative and response begins after the first major switch in the novel, from the Casaubon–Dorothea–Celia–James story to the Featherstone–Fred sequence which begins, in effect, in chapter 11. In chapter 12 Featherstone takes the initiative of requiring Fred to produce an exculpatory letter from Bulstrode (his uncle). Fred responds (ch. 13) by asking his father to ask for such a letter. The father does so, Bulstrode asks advice of his wife, she responds with favour, Bulstrode then responds to Vincy's initiative by supplying a letter. In chapter 14 Fred responds to Featherstone's initiative in 12 by taking him the letter that he required. At this point, another and overlapping initiative and response continuity becomes prominent. Linked by proximate continuity of the cast to the scene in chapter 13 between Vincy and Bulstrode is the immediately preceding scene between Lydgate and Bulstrode, in which the latter takes the initiative of telling Lydgate that he wants to see Tyke appointed to the hospital chaplaincy. The response to this occurs in chapter 18, where Lydgate, when provoked, implements Bulstrode's requirement by voting for his man.

Continuities of initiative and response can extend over long spans. There is a continuity from chapter 8 right across to 28, because it is in 28 we learn that Celia's response to Sir James's 'little attentions' was to accept him. Featherstone's response to the reassuring letter that Fred brings him in chapter 14 is not only to give him £100 in the same chapter, but to try to burn the second will in chapter 33. But here, we encounter the obvious alternative to a response which satisfies the initiative: Featherstone's initiative is to ask Mary Garth to give him his will-box, and her response is to refuse. But the sequence extends further. Mary's response works also as initiative from Caleb's point of view. Her scrupulousness over the will puts Fred Vincy at a disadvantage. Caleb's response to it is therefore to decide that he has an obligation to help Fred – this is made explicit in his conversation with his wife in chapter 40 – and then, when in 56 Fred takes the initiative of asking to work under Caleb, Caleb's response is at once to agree. An important further point is that in the conversation between Caleb and Susan Garth in chapter 40, we find Caleb's affirmative response to the initiative Sir James formed in 38 – to ask Caleb to manage his own estate and also Mr Brooke's. This in its turn is only Sir James's response, or part of it, to Brooke's initiative in inviting Will Ladislaw to stay with him so as to edit the 'Middlemarch Pioneer' in chapter 30 and Will's response in accepting – which transpires from Brooke's conversation in 34. Casaubon's response to Brooke's initiative comes in chapter 37 and is to write to Will attempting to forbid him to agree; to which Will's response, also in 37, is to repudiate Casaubon's injunction. Continuities of initiative and response have by now inter-connected the whole Garth-family/Fred Vincy story with the story of Dorothea, Casaubon and Will.

Another similar example of continuity achieved through the initiative–response process comes in chapter 41, where Raffles' initiative is to call on Joshua Rigg Featherstone to beg from him. Rigg throws him out. Raffles' response to this is to take the initiative of coming again, this time to look for Bulstrode (ch. 53), and he also seeks Bulstrode out on a second visit (ch. 61), when he takes the initiative of telling him that Will is the son of the woman Bulstrode wronged long ago, and of telling Will about her also (ch. 60). Bulstrode responds by offering Will an allowance, (ch. 61), but in response to this and also Raffles' giving the information to himself Will rejects the allowance. Bulstrode responds to Raffles' next initiative, however, by defiance (ch. 68). I omit certain of the later details; but at the closing stages of this continuity it is Bulstrode's initiative (ch. 60), in offering to lend Lydgate £1000, and Lydgate's response of acceptance, which largely bring about the resolution of the Lydgate–Rosamond story; and it is the double initiative which Dorothea decides to take when she learns of this – first to offer Lydgate a way out of his obligation to Bulstrode by replacing the loan from him by a loan from her (ch. 76), and second to call on Rosamond (ch. 77), which brings about the resolution of the Dorothea–Will Ladislaw story as well (ch. 83). Once again, the patterns of initiative and response establish long-extending continuities within the various major strands of the narrative, and also establish continuities between these strands.

Perhaps the most decisive of all these initiative–response continuities is also a short and inconspicuous one. It does not begin until chapter 80, with Miss Henrietta Noble's 'inarticulate little sounds', the 'beaver-like notes' of distress that she makes as she searches for her lozenge-box. Mr Farebrother's response is a double one: first to find the box, and then to explain to his guest Dorothea how Miss Henrietta has formed a deep 'attachment' to Will who gave it her. The importance of the sequence transpires in chapter 83. Will comes to Lowick Court and asks to see Dorothea. She feels a difficulty: 'she could not receive him . . . where her husband's prohibition seemed to dwell' (and) 'she shrank from going out to him'. But Will has responded to Henrietta Noble's attachment to him by the initiative of asking her to come with him and make the request on his behalf. Dorothea's response to Henrietta Noble's initiative is to ask Will in. We know, doubtless, that the meeting will come about somehow. The novelist's problem is how to arrange this within the *convenances* of Middlemarch society. The initiative–response continuity from chapters 80 to 83 does not only connect and establish a further continuity between the story of Dorothea and the Farebrother household; also it is this link which makes it possible to resolve Dorothea's story.

I have omitted, for the moment, one important aspect of the Henrietta Noble–Will–Dorothea sequence, because before I refer to it, there may be a need to distinguish some linked pairs of events from the pattern of initiative-and-response linkage. Certain linked pairs, such as 'Will buys a horse in the backstreets of Houndsley' (ch. 23), 'Will catches typhoid and is ill' (ch. 26), and many others, cannot be seen as initiative–response, but illustrate what George Eliot refers to in chapter 61 as 'the train of *causes* into which he had locked himself'. It is not always obvious whether a pair of events are better seen as initiative–response or as cause–effect. For example, a direct sequel of Dorothea's accepting Casaubon is that Mrs Cadwallader tells Sir James that Celia likes him. Which of the two processes is that? Perhaps it depends on how much we see Mrs Cadwallader in the rôle of matchmaker.

The more we do so, the more the initiative–response process seems in point.

This is perhaps because in several respects there is a more defined outline or structure when we see a sequence as initiative–response. The initiative by one character directly poses the question of what some other character or characters will do. The characters in question are specifiable, they have distinct positions and rôles; and what they can do in response is limited and specifiable too. In chapter 58 Lydgate tells Rosamond of their money difficulties. If there is to be a response it must be from her. That she should ask her father is one out of a circumscribed set of possible responses. Often the set has two members only – agreement, refusal – as here. Refusals of course comprise several of the decisive events in the narrative. Later (ch. 64) Lydgate places the house in the agent's hands for sale, Rosamond's response is to call and withdraw it. Then, she writes to Sir Godwin, whose response (ch. 65) is to decline to help. When Lydgate reads Sir Godwin's letter, he has no course left but to ask Bulstrode (ch. 67).

These summaries are less banal than they may seem: because they introduced, in passing, additional features of the processes of continuity, and these can perhaps now be identified. First the point omitted about Henrietta Noble may be raised afresh. In fact, there are two points. George Eliot did not, I am glad to say, delay until chapter 80 to reveal Henrietta Noble's regard for Will. Already in chapter 50 Lydgate had mentioned this, and mentioned it to Dorothea. That scene closed with Dorothea's reflecting on how Will would indeed have been kindly, and perhaps also a little forebearing, with the old lady. What follows?

Really, that certain items of information about Will, about Dorothea, and about Dorothea's knowledge of Will and also Henrietta Noble are *deposited* for us. Then, in chapter 80, what Dorothea knows is re-activated or *confirmed* both for her and for us; and finally, in 83 these items are what might be referred to as *called in*. That is to say, Dorothea responds as she does to Henrietta Noble's initiative, not by virtue of the initiative alone, but by virtue of that initiative taken in the light of Dorothea's pre-established knowledge of Henrietta Noble's devotion to Will and his kindnesses to her. Similarly at every point in the narrative, events that occur also deposit, for the characters themselves often, but always for the reader, items of knowledge about the agents or others, and about the characters' insight into themselves or each other.

The second point about the Henrietta Noble sequence in chapter 80 is of precisely this kind, and if anything more important. Dorothea might have rebuffed Henrietta Noble had it not been that the scene after dinner brings her to the realization of the 'Oh, I did love him!' that she comes out with when she gets home that night. She now knows the full truth about herself. That it is the truth, and that she knows it for the truth, are deposited for the reader, to be called in three chapters later.

Surely, these processes of *depositing, confirming*, and *calling in* are at work, and massively, all the time. Much of the deposits are extremely basic in kind, and the individual novel has not needed to deposit them – women attract men, so does money, characters are not deaf, scholars over forty-five are likely to be old sticks, societies have forms of integration, etc. etc. Processes of depositing within the development of the novel are for more individualized purposes: Will is Casaubon's second cousin, Fred is already nearly affianced to Mary, and so on. Collectively, these deposits are altogether essential to its narrative. The reader would not accept it that Sir James begins to pay small attentions to Celia simply because Mrs Cadwallader tells him that Celia likes him. We need to know already that Celia has charm enough for this to happen, given that Sir James is the kind of man we have had it deposited for us that he is. So likewise at every point. Every continuity-process is made possible by a combination, a collaboration, between the prior member of the initiative–response or cause–effect pair, and the massed deposits which constitute the voluminous background to our reading of the book. Furthermore, those deposits, if made over-far back, periodically require what I have referred to as a process of being confirmed (to continue the banking metaphor, this process is remarkably like a periodic revaluation of someone's holdings), if they are to be readily available to be called on; and of course confirmation, or re-affirmation, of many things at once is going on implicitly all the time that the novel is progressing in a consistent manner, almost regardless of what is occurring in detail.

I said just now that there came a point when Lydgate 'had no course left' but to seek help from Bulstrode, or that 'Dorothea might have rebuffed Henrietta Noble' had something not been the case which was the case: implying thereby that in the juncture which in fact occurred she barely could have done other than she did. These two points bring forward a further suggestion about the narrative processes in *Middlemarch* and the continuities that they create in it. Whether initiatives or otherwise, events in a narrative do not occur so as to be wholly closed within themselves save for their specific sequel. Normally they raise possibilities, and *more possibilities than one*, of what will eventuate from them. Frequently, perhaps in the last analysis always, these possibilities are directly or indirectly of a binary nature. To cite one example only, every request or demand raises the twin possibility that it will be acceded to, or that it will be refused. In chapter one I used the Scots word to 'propone' – to put forward for consideration – for the various possibilities of sequel which arise from the action in this way; and we could speak of the items *proponed* by the action step by step, or we could call these items *suppositions*.

Clearly, what is proponed in this way is another kind of 'deposit', but it is quite different in kind from the deposits of information mentioned earlier on. For example, when Caleb Garth in chapter 40 receives Sir James's letter, what is deposited or confirmed are many items about his own character, education, and so on, and about others also: 'His face had an expression of grave surprise. . . .' 'He did not like to be questioned while he was reading'; 'Brooke didn't like to ask me himself, I can see. . .' 'Here is an honour to your father, children'; 'Mind you ask fair pay, Caleb'; 'and then with a little start of remembrance he said, "Mary, write and give up that school. . ."' What is 'proponed', however, is a number of possibilities of future development. Caleb may still refuse, on some sudden scruple; he may accept for Freshitt but not for Tipton; he may accept both; then if Mary is not to go away, she may still marry Fred; or, might she marry someone else? – maybe Farebrother? – 'It's a thousand pities Christy didn't take to business, Susan. I shall want help by-and-by'. Who will Caleb get to help him? Well, it is in the very next chapter that Raffles is introduced. Who knows? Even that development is not quite out of the question at first. As we read, the suppositions proliferate more or less definitely in our minds. No one, of course, will long wonder whether Raffles will end up as Caleb's lieutenant. But this is only to say that along with how the events of the narrative continually propone for the future, they also continually *eliminate* from among what has been proponed already.

This is what lies behind the junctures involving Lydgate and Dorothea that I mentioned earlier on. When in chapter 63 Lydgate refuses help from Farebrother, the possibility that his difficulties may be solved through such help is eliminated both by his refusal and by the deposited fact that in any case Farebrother probably did not have the resources to help him adequately. When Rosamond countermands Lydgate's instructions to Trumbull the agent, the possibility that the Lydgates can move into a smaller house is eliminated, or virtually so (why the whole process might not simply be gone through over again invites reflection, but the reason is there). Early in chapter 70 we read of Bulstrode's watching by the half-conscious, half-delirious Raffles. 'He could not but see the death of Raffles, and see in it his own deliverance. What was the removal of this wretched creature?' What is proposed is obvious; but when Bulstrode hands over the patient to Mrs Abel, the supposition is eliminated, and the elimination is quite sharp and specific. When Mrs Abel tells Bulstrode that if he is too mean to give Raffles a tot from his own stock, she and her husband will spare him something to drink from their own meagre supply, the possibility that Bulstrode will continue to refuse is eliminated, unless he at once tells her the full reason why. When he gives her the key to the wine-cooler, that eliminates both his being open, and Raffles' getting well.

What I should like in the end to propose is the conception which we might call that of a *narrative member*. This conception seems to be of what we ought probably to see as the minimum unit by means of which the totality of any narrative is extended and continued. It is impossible to think that merely the event-in-the-narrative is this unit, because (as must by now have transpired) the totality of a narrative is greatly more than the totality of events in the narrative. A narrative member, as I conceive it, comprises in the first place either any initiative and the response to it, or a cause and its effect. I shall call these its *primary pair*. Second, it comprises items of information, including evaluation, which involve the characters' understanding of each other or of themselves, and likewise our understanding of them and their situation. I see these items as either *deposited*, or re-activated and *confirmed*, by the primary pair; and furthermore, see these also as *calling in* certain other deposits which have been established at earlier stages of the novel, and re-activated from time to time. Finally, the narrative member comprises those suppositions which are proposed by the primary pair. Putting all this in more general terms, it amounts simply to the fact that the reading experience of a novel comprises the *events that happen* in it, the mass of more general *understanding* about the whole situation that the reader constantly builds up and constantly draws on as he makes the developments intelligible to himself; and the much more fluid mass of *possibilities*, possibilities which enter his mind as there grows up in it Johnson's 'restless and unquenchable' curiosity as to the sequel, and which are progressively eliminated by the second members of primary pairs as these arrive throughout the novel.

All in all, this means that the narrative member would comprise three kinds of item and various specific relations between them: relations for which I have suggested such names as depositing, confirming or re-activating, calling in, proponing and eliminating. Between the two members of the primary pair is of course another relation, the familiar one that we might refer to by some such expression as 'ensues in' or the like. A narrative member would itself therefore be a complex of several kinds of item and several kinds of relation between those items. My suggestion is that from the standpoint of structure we get the best idea of the totality of a narrative if we think of it as a combination of units of this complex kind. There is in fact one very large omission here, which I have hinted at, but no more. It is the enormous body of presuppositions, of several kinds, that we bring to the reading of any work – *from outside it.*

In what ways, I ask finally, does identifying the complex I have called a narrative member relate to the matter of continuity which I began by discussing? I see three ways. First, as must have become obvious already, the second member of the primary pair very frequently becomes the first member of a subsequent pair; and the members which are successive stages of any such strand of the whole narrative – 'part of the novel' – (The story of Dorothea, the story of Raffles, etc.) simply overlap. Second, the deposits which are 'called in' or the suppositions which are eliminated within any given member are commonly not deposited, nor proponed, in the narrative interval between the primary pair in that member. This is quite obvious. They often date from long before, they belong to the whole progressing mass of the novel. But this fact means that in the chronology of the narrative, the narrative members overlap much more densely and far-reachingly than they do by virtue only of how the second member of one primary pair will become the first member of a second. Third, the narrative members which successively embody one 'part of the novel' (as I used the phrase just now) of course overlap directly with those embodying other parts. Widely, they do so partly of course because of the extensive gaps in 'continuity of the cast' discussed earlier. The Casaubons set out for Rome in chapter 10 and return in 19; with, in between, several narrative members involving the Fred Vincy part of the novel or the Lydgate–Rosamond part. They do so more widely still, by virtue of the great spans over which the deposits remain available for 'calling in' (Brooke's demerits as a landlord are first indicated in chapter 2, and 'called in' decisively in 39); or again the great spans between a supposition's being proposed, and its being eliminated, or alternatively its eventuating. The major suppositions in *Middlemarch* ('Lydgate's marriage may end in disaster', 'Dorothea may marry Will in the end' and so on) extend over nearly the whole work. I think that if we could really enumerate the succession of the narrative members, and the constituent items in each, then the whole set of members would define the narrative structure of a book. I cannot believe this impossible in principle, but the inextricable density of the overlapping, and the complexity of indirect continuities which result, are reflections of its at least decisive difficulty in practice.

4

Identity, inversion and density elements in narrative: three tales by Chekhov, James and Lawrence

I

'Now *mythos* is actually the arrangement and combination of the actions' (Aristotle says) 'just as character is the name given to what makes the agents what they are; and thought, to passages where the characters are speaking and they advance arguments or express opinions' (*Poetics*, vi.8). This essay advances some points that may be made about narrative structure in fiction of a certain rather distinctive kind: a kind increasingly important over the past hundred years or so, in which it might be said, *almost nothing happens.*

Discussion of narrative structure has often concentrated on works like the folk-tale, or the tales of Boccaccio and the like, or other fictions where the 'arrangement and combination of the actions' look all the time like the predominant organizing principle. There is another kind of fiction, which gives an equally strong impression of plan and organization – perhaps a greater – but at the same time suggests throughout that that organization operates quite otherwise than through the 'action', the 'what happens'. This is a familiar fact, but how to take stock of it is less so.

Anything whatever in a fiction can be treated as the 'what happens' of that fiction. The kind of narrative now to be considered often includes *conversations* between the characters that are especially prominent and important: and of course there is a sense in which a conversation is an event, is part of the 'what happens' of the narrative. Moreover, even if it is recognized that there is, or can be, a significant difference between conversations and other events in a narrative, in that other events are likely to change the whole situation in a narrative as conversations often do not, it remains the case that some conversations in narrative can be, or at least can include, events of the greatest and most obvious substantiality. Estrangements, for example, can occur during conversation and can be substantial events in the most straightforward sense. So would most events of the kind Aristotle calls 'recognition', anagnorisis.

But there is one conspicuously distinctive feature of conversations in narrative. It may be expressed by saying that, in comparison with events of most other kinds, conversations are in principle readily, and in practice regularly, *cancellable*. What this means in full will become clear in the course of the discussion, but in general terms it means that a conversation may terminate, and the situation in the novel be, at least ostensibly, the same as if it had not occurred. Episodes in a narrative other than conversations may be of this same kind, and (as was mentioned above) conversations can sometimes have quite another kind of significance and substantiality. Being a conversation-episode is neither a necessary, nor a sufficient condition for being 'cancellable' in this sense. For all that, it does often seem to be rather distinctive of conversations in a narrative that they can have a beginning, and an ending, and in a certain sense the second of these simply undoes the first. Our interest in the situation in the book, or our comprehension of it, may have become much greater than it was before; but we should hardly know how to say that as a result of the conversation anything in that situation had changed.

Consider Chekhov's *A Boring Story*. Some of the conversation-episodes in this narrative are clearly 'cancelled' as the narrative proceeds. One example of this would be the early-morning 'sample' conversation between Nikolai and his wife: another, that at breakfast between himself and his daughter. It is convenient, because of what follows, to tabulate these episodes:[1]

Ref. no.	Episode opens	Events (if any) in the episode	Cancellation
A	p. 48: 'the day begins for me with the coming in of my wife'	None ('and all this in a tone of voice as if she were telling me something new')	p. 50: 'she goes away at last'
B	p. 50: 'my daughter Lisa comes in'	None ('I am as cold as ice cream, and I feel ashamed')	p. 51: Nikolai leaves the house

1. Page-references are to the editions cited at the end of this chapter.

Perhaps Nikolai's lecture (pp. 51–8) may also be regarded as a conversation-piece (one-sided, as most lectures are) of rather the same kind. Certainly it is presented as occurring without the least significant effect upon anything that 'happens' in the narrative.

There are other conversation-episodes which in the end prove to be like those above, though ostensibly they are not so. These are episodes in which some substantial change and development in the whole situation is indeed introduced; only, having been introduced or proposed, *it is then rejected* by the course that the conversation takes:

C	p. 59: a student calls	The student requests Nikolai to 'pass' him.	Nikolai refuses
D(i)	p. 61: a young doctor calls	He requests a research topic	Nikolai refuses
D(ii)	Nikolai in the end agrees	–	The resulting research is 'boring' and 'useless'
E	p. 97: Nikolai's ward Katya arrives during the night	She begs Nikolai to take her money for himself	He refuses and Katya goes away
F	p. 98: Katya comes to see Nikolai in his hotel at Kharkov	She begs Nikolai to advise her what to do	Nikolai says he cannot, and she leaves

There is also a third context in which the process here called 'cancellation' can occur. In these cases the element of cancellation does not occur in dialogue but outside it, in the course of the narrative. Such cases are frequent in *A Boring Story*

G	p. 62: (narrative by Nikolai about the earlier life of Katya)	'One fine day . . . Katya joined a theatrical company and went away . . . to Ufa'	p. 67: 'After spending about a year in the Crimea, *she came back home*'
H	(embedded within G above)	Katya has a love-affair and bears a child.	(Katya's letter) 'I have been cruelly deceived . . . yesterday I buried my child'

Ref. no.	Episode opens	Events (if any) in the episode	Cancellation
I	p. 94: direct narration	Lisa is ill in the night	p. 97: she recovers ('but the moans upstairs ceased')
J	(embedded in I above)	'I stood thinking what to prescribe for Lisa'	'and I decided to prescribe nothing'
K	p. 74: direct narration: Nikolai visits Katya	p. 85: 'I vow never to go and see Katya again'	'though I know very well that I will go to her again the next day'

II

It is possible to see a certain general analogy between the set of items composing a fiction, and the set of items comprising a *group* in the mathematical sense. One of the properties of a group is that for any operation which may be performed in respect of two members of the group (addition, say, or multiplication) there is an 'inverse element' which – to put the matter simply – will bring you back where you started: for example, if you multiply by n, and then multiply by $1/n$. Similarly for another mathematical operation, that of addition, with n and $-n$. With this idea in mind, we could suggest a level at which organization is created in a narrative by recurrent reliance upon 'inverse elements' effecting a kind of cancellation, and giving a recurrent sense that the reader is 'back where he started'.

It seems that this conception may well be important for some narratives. If, for example, the three tabulations above are amalgamated in proper sequence as they occur in the text, something remarkable emerges. It is, that (along with one or two other, minor examples of the same thing) they comprise virtually the whole of that text from the beginning through to the end. It may even be suggested that there is a distinctive kind of narrative episode, which is best defined as what is introduced by an item that is subsequently followed by another item standing as an inverse element to the first one, and thereby concluding the episode: in effect 'cancelling' it, because there is a quite meaningful sense in which the situation in the narrative is 'back where it started'.

If this definition were adopted, it would lead to an analysis by which some episodes would partially or wholly be embedded in others, but there is nothing against such a conception of 'episode', and a significant fact now presents itself. Some narratives may doubtless be seen as consisting of episodes organized in this way: but not all can. Therefore, to say that a certain narrative has this kind of organization is not tautologous but a point of substance. Some narratives have little or no element of constantly bringing the reader 'back where he started': they press forward through intrigue and climax to their resolution and end; while others introduce, perhaps very prominently, 'inverse elements' of this kind.

Cancellation is not often present in a narrative as conspicuously and persistently as it is in *A Boring Story*; but on the other hand, that narrative is not unique. Of course, even in *A Boring Story*, there are some items in the narrative which have no inverse element to cancel them, and which we should want to regard as in some sense significant parts of the 'action' of the *nouvelle*. Nikolai (at least if we may accept his own intimation of this) approaches near to the end of his life; his daughter Lisa secretly marries a man who is probably an adventurer; and Katya apparently goes back to her old life among the demirep society of the Crimea. But all of those events are left half-hypothetical ('probably', 'apparently') and as it were peripheral: they are simply not the real point. The story is 'boring' in the first place because it is part of the life of the teller to see it as such. At another level it is boring because it depicts a whole society of waste and pointlessness. Those 'significant parts of the action' can be left to some extent, hypothetical, because they come more as specimens and illustrations of this mode of life than as really confirming it for what it is. At another level again, of course *A Boring Story* is not boring at all, immeasurably not.

I should like now to consider Lawrence's *Love Among the Haystacks* from this point of view. In *Love Among the Haystacks*, there are events which are significant in that it is they which give the narrative its final meaning. Paula becomes engaged to Maurice, Lydia parts company with her 'slouching parasitic' husband and joins Maurice's brother Geoffrey, and the tale unquestionably indicates that these two events lead towards a third, which is the reconciliation of the brothers out of the antagonism between them at the start. These three events are much more than illustration; they are the culmination and resolution of the story.

At the same time, in *Love Among the Haystacks* the operation of inverse elements is surprisingly prominent. The way that, as the brothers work at the haystack, the loaded hay-waggon rides up (p. 11) and then goes away again (p. 13; left to be understood) seems to be representative of the rhythms of the earlier part of the tale.

Maurice, for example, falls over the edge of the stack (p. 14) and at first seems to be seriously hurt: but that proves to be wrong ('it's not hurt me', p. 17; 'there's nowt ails me'. p. 19). The German girl runs over from the Vicarage (p. 14) and accuses Geoffrey: but no one believes what she says, the accusation peters out, and she simply goes back again (p. 20) as if she had not come. She then comes to the field a second time, with some special food for the 'invalid' (p. 21); but it is not needed, and she goes back once again (p. 25). The 'seedy, slinking' tramp joins the group at lunch time (p. 22), and then leaves it (p. 25). Within this incident his wife arrives, but takes nothing to eat and before long goes away in her turn (p. 25).

Something of course does happen in the course of these incidents: the stack gets a little higher, lunch is eaten, the father learns the German girl's name, the tramp's wife notes a possible sleeping-place for the night. Other and more important points than these are also steadily being made, and the discussion will turn to them in due course. But none of this is like what happens when Geoffrey asks the tramp's wife to go to Canada with him, and she agrees. In the earlier stages of the story, and at a certain level, or in a certain sense, each of the episodes noticed above returns the reader to where he started. 'Nothing really happens'.

III

Prima facie, such a mode of organization is perplexing. One supposes that in the fiction at least of major writers of fiction every single part of the text has some necessary function, even if a subordinate one; the very idea of an inverse element, of something in a text which can have the effect of cancelling out some earlier part of that text and of returning the reader to where he was earlier still, seems at first to be contrary to that principle. It may be helpful at this point, though, to notice that in every episode of these narratives (and of course of others) the text contains a great deal which at the level of action that has been under consideration hitherto, appears to have *no relevance whatever*. Perhaps another analogy with the mathematical conditions required for the existence of a group may, for some readers anyhow, throw this point into relief: though in this case there is less of an analogy than the previous one. What these latter items in the text somewhat resemble is not the inverse but the 'identity' element in a mathematical group. To take the most familiar case: when they are progressively added to the text in the act of writing or of reading, it is somewhat like multiplying by $(+1)$: a further operation is carried out, but the whole is unchanged. (This analogy is obviously incomplete, because a mathematical group is required to have a *unique* identity element – for example, $+1$ – to which I see no parallel in the case of a text.)

Consider more closely the episode in *Love Among the Haystacks* in which Paula runs over to the 'injured' Maurice, lying on the ground, and accuses Geoffrey of having pushed him off the top of the haystack. From what the novelist has told him in direct narrative already, the reader knows that this is as good as true. If the other characters in the tale were to believe it, the narrative would presumably have to take another turn; but on the contrary, they brush it casually and good-humouredly aside. Again, if Paula did not return to the Vicarage but became betrothed on the spot to Maurice and went back with him to the farm, that would also make the story take another turn; but she does not. However, at the level of alternatives such as these, much of the information contained in the text – though of course it seems paradoxical to say this while other levels of narrative organization await discussion – *make no difference*. They operate like 'identity elements' in relation to the episode in which they occur. Thus we read that the German girl's speech in English made a strange, 'passionate' sing-song; that when the men heard how she began to cry, it 'made the animal bristle within them'; that she sounded 'shrill and vindictive'; that she knelt beside Maurice's head, and let her bosom press against him when she helped him up; that the Vicar was 'asking for explanations' and sounded 'slightly disappointed' when he examined Maurice and found him unhurt; that he was a 'pale, rather cold man' and hated Paula; that Geoffrey was deeply shaken and abashed at the thought of what he had done; and a very great deal else of this kind.

Yet at a certain level, none of all this 'makes any difference'. None of it seems to have any bearing, at the level of significant action in this episode which has been under discussion, and might be diagrammatized as follows:

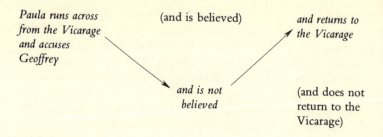

Paula runs across
from the Vicarage
and accuses
Geoffrey

(and is believed)

and returns to
the Vicarage

and is not
believed

(and does not
return to the
Vicarage)

Every one of the items listed at the end of the last paragraph could be different, and not only could the train of 'significant action' equally well run just as it does, but also, equally well, could Lawrence have adopted any of the other possibilities in the diagram ('and is believed and returns'; 'and is believed and does not return'). Moreover, it is obvious that in every episode there are a great many such 'identity' items. Thus, in the later episode where Geoffrey and Lydia come together, we read 'she fell to gently stroking his hair, with timid, pleading finger-tips'. Lydia might have done this, and Geoffrey not invited her to go with him; or not done it, and he might still have invited her. Whereas, if she had not come back at all, he could neither have made his proposal to her, nor refrained from making it.

There is an interesting point about these elements which function like identity elements in relation to the episode in which they occur. It has already become clear that there is a sense in which items functioning as *inverse* elements (Nikolai rejects the request of the student, who then goes away; 'after spending about a year in the Crimea . . . [Katya] came back home . . .'; 'I decided not to prescribe anything . . .'; Maurice proves to be unharmed from the fall) *make the episode in which they occur like an identity element in the fiction as a whole.* That is what is implied by saying 'we are back where we started'. But, these items that produce the inverting-operation seem not to invert everything within the episode that they terminate and, at one level, cancel. It is quite surprising and interesting to see what they do not operate upon in this way. What they do not operate on in this way are, specifically, *the elements which function as identity elements with respect to the episode in which they themselves occur.*

There is thus a kind of stratification of the narrative. The argument was, that many items which occurred in the text of this or that episode were supernumerary to it at the level of straight-forward 'significant action'. They did not bear at all upon whether the episode terminated in one way or in another; nor upon whether it underwent an inversion-operation or not. So they could be likened to identity elements. Yet at the same time, these are precisely the elements which are independent of the 'inverse' element which terminates the episode. For example: the episode in which Paula accuses Geoffrey is 'cancelled out' in respect of that accusation, and the story progresses, at a certain level, just as if the accusation had never been made. But all the same, the information released in the episode about Paula's feelings and personality, about what the Vicar is like, about what Geoffrey has gone through and how he may therefore have changed or be now susceptible of change, has not been subject to the operation of the inverse element. Every one of those items retains, as it were, its full potency, its full operativeness in the story.

If that is so, then one of two things follows. Either, these elements in a sense supererogatory to the episode in which they occur, have no integral function whatever in the narrative and are simply decorative or digressive (which is contrary to the hypothesis that we are examining the fiction of a major writer); or, the series of episodes in narratives of this general kind sets up what might be termed a 'ground-floor' level of organization, and the items supernumerary to that must progressively create and contribute to (let us say) a 'first-floor' level, precisely to the extent that they are not intrinsic to the ground floor level of organization and are not 'cancelled' by the inverse element which, at that level, cancels out the episode in which they occur.

If this train of thought is right, we are provided with not an impressionistic but a systematic basis upon which two distinct (though doubtless related) organizations may be distinguished within a narrative, and individual items allocated to one or other of them; and in fiction of the particular kind that this discussion has been concentrating upon, we may say that the organization in a series of episodes seems in large part to be for a quite distinctive purpose. That purpose would appear to be, to contain and release (perhaps in such contexts as satisfy prevailing literary conventions like conventional length for narratives of various *genres*, or fictional 'realism', or something like James's 'density of specification', and so on) items which the reader can sense to be independent of that first level of organization, and therefore which can contribute to, and help to create, another perhaps less obvious one.

IV

A possible name for those items in a narrative which function like identity elements in respect of the episode in which they occur, and which are themselves not subject to the inverse-element effect as discussed above, would be simply *density-items*. In narratives such as the two discussed up to this point, they are obviously very numerous. They constitute easily the major bulk of the text as a whole.

But on reflection, they prove very much not to be all of one single kind. A preliminary distinction must be made before this point is taken further. Consider James's *Lesson of the Master*. In this *nouvelle* the series of episodes might be outlined something like this:

A1 Paul Overt arrives at Summersoft, the big country house, and converses with General Fancourt (pages 109–13), and Mrs St George (114–18)

A2 He is introduced to Marian Fancourt and converses with her (pp. 118–26)

A3 He converses, in the smoking room, with St George himself (pp. 129–38)

A4 He meets Marian Fancourt and St George at a gallery in Bond Street, and converses with them (pp. 139–42)

A5 He calls at Marian's house (pp. 142–7)

A6 He dines with the St Georges (pp. 149–63).

[A7 He goes abroad, writes a new novel, and after two years' absence returns (pp. 163–6)]

A8 Shortly after his return, he meets General Fancourt and they converse (pp. 167–70)

A9 That same evening he calls at Manchester Square and converses with St George (pp. 170–5)

This banal catalogue brings out an interesting fact. Save for item 7 above, the episodes into which the *nouvelle* naturally divides are all conversation-episodes (the Jamesian 'scene'); and easily most of these conversation-episodes terminate in items which function as 'inverse' elements. This does not hold of the last episode, because that leaves Paul and St George more or less estranged; nor perhaps of the last but one, of which it could be said that it leaves Paul both distressed and disquieted. These may be seen as events in the action. Other events such as Paul's falling in love with Marian, or as episode 7 above, cannot really be said to be related to any of the conversation-episodes in at all the same direct way, and it is difficult to say that any 'action' takes place specifically in any of the earlier conversations. The characters come together and talk, there is a transmission of opinions and information, and then each episode is terminated by the inverse item separating the interlocutors who have come together to make the episode in question. Episode 7, Paul's sojourn abroad, is also terminated by an event (his return) which is really an inverse event, since once he is back in London he reverts – at least until the close of the story – to his old life of visits, meetings, conversations. 'We are back where we started'.

Released, however, from within the sequence of conversations, there is another sequence, a sequence of events or actions in a quite straightforward sense. These events do not occur within the episodes above, though nearly all of them come to the reader's knowledge because they are *reported* within those episodes. This series of events, and the occasions of their release to the reader, may be summarized as follows:

B1	Paul falls in love with Marian	reported in conversation A3, and confirmed in an authorial comment in the course of A5 (p. 146)
B2	St George persuades Paul to give up thoughts of marriage 'and to write'	narrated after A6 as a result of it ('it is not a perversion of the truth to pronounce that encounter the direct cause of his departure' p. 163)
B3	Paul goes abroad, lives alone and writes a new novel	narrated in A7
B4	Mrs St George dies	reported in the course of A7 (Marian's letter to Paul)
B5	St George becomes engaged to Marian	reported in conversation, A8
B6	St George gives up writing (?)	reported in conversation A9
B7	Paul and St George become (temporarily?) estranged	presented in A9, at close

B8	Paul publishes his new book.	narrated after A9 (author's concluding summary)

The events in series A above are the conversation-episodes that are presented directly and at length in the novel; but (with the partial exception of A9) they all conclude with an inverse element, and directly, they are in no way the stages in the fiction between the initial situation of the characters and its terminal situation. These stages are in fact represented by series B; but *none* of the items in this series (I call them 'items', for it is of course the whole point that they are not 'episodes') is presented directly – again with the partial exception of the estrangement between Paul and St George at the end. Yet if it is the items in series B that mark the stages between initial and terminal situation, that is so only in a limiting sense: for in principle, this series could stand as the series of events in many different possible narratives, including narratives, one might almost say, that James would have died sooner than write.

The further items, in the narrative as a whole, that supplement and modify series B, and make it into the particular narrative it in fact is, are extremely numerous; and once again, in bulk make up easily the greatest part of the text. These items are identity elements *vis-à-vis* the episodes in series A in which they occur; and (as we saw) the inverse elements that cancel the episodes of series A leave them uncancelled and unaffected.

Also, they themselves can never be inverse elements for any member of series B, which is a way of saying that they are not 'events' in the familiar sense. Here, in tabular form for convenience, are a very few of these items, in *The Lesson of the Master*.

Item	occurs in	page no.
St George is a 'distinguished' [novelist]... a 'high literary figure'	A1	109, 110
Paul is a 'young aspirant' but 'even morbid modesty might view the authorship of Ginistrella as constituting a degree of identity'	A1	110
'some of St George's books are "of a queerness" . . . *as he knows* . . . he doesn't esteem them . . .'	A2	123
Paul is 'wonderfully on the right road'	A6	153

Item	occurs in	page no.
St George considers himself 'a successful charlatan', 'perfect Philistine'	A7	166
St George's performance had been 'infirm', his 'vein' is 'exhausted'	A6, A9	
Paul's new novel is 'really magnificent'	A9	

The above is of course only a selection from what makes up the 'density' of the *nouvelle*. But that density, and intricacy, is also increased by something distinctive: the ways in which the author makes the implications of such items problematical. That Paul, for example, is 'wonderfully on the right road' is what St George says. But other items, which could be arranged in an independent series, bear intricately upon this and all that is like it. Here is merely one such (Marian and Paul are conversing):

> 'St. George talked a great deal about your book. He says it's really important.'
>
> – 'Important? Ah the grand creature' – Paul groaned for joy.
>
> – 'He was wonderfully amusing, he was inexpressibly droll, while we walked about. . .'

The point is, does St George's 'drolling' *cancel* the claim to importance? Similarly over the last item in the catalogue above, when one looks at the full text:

> When Paul's new book came out . . . Mr and Mrs St George found it really magnificent.

Was it 'really magnificent'? James does not quite say. The St Georges may no longer be altogether the judges. If they were, would 'really magnificent' be quite how they would express the matter?

St George himself spends much time in putting forward a way in which to understand such items as are catalogued above:

> – 'one's children interfere with perfection . . . Marriage interferes'
>
> – 'You think then the artist shouldn't marry? . . . Not even when his wife's in sympathy with his work?'
>
> – 'She never is – she can't be'

From the point of view of the narrative as a whole, if that is gospel truth, then the items in that catalogue are all to be taken at face value, and the question of possible irony does not arise. But is that the case? Further items again may easily be read as casting doubt on: 'She never is – she can't be', and the rest. James does a great deal to suggest that the second Mrs St George was in these respects quite different from the first. Here are some examples of this 'great deal'.

Item	occurs in	page no.
Mrs St George once made her husband burn a book ('about myself') that she thought bad, and says he has been very lazy	A1	115
Marian is 'an artistic intelligence of the first order'	A3	136
Mrs St George does not allow her husband to smoke or drink	A4	130, 138
Marian has 'liberal humanity' and discusses 'with extreme seriousness' the 'high theme of perfection'	A5	143, 145

In the end, the question is left open. There is some suggestion at the close of the narrative that St George might one day write a new and better book, though in fact it is not written within the span of this *nouvelle*.

It seems possible that the two tools of analysis made use of so far in this discussion, and suggesting that it is possible systematically to distinguish several different 'layers' in these narratives, might be taken a step further; for if we think about all the array of 'items' such as 'supplement and modify series B' (p. 64 above) and have just been illustrated by a number of examples, we could suggest that some of these function as identity elements, and some as inverse elements, *vis-à-vis* others. To put the matter in this way is of course to ignore all the nuances and subtleties that in fact make up the staple of our pleasure and preoccupation as we read. Some will see it as a crude relegation of everything of meaning and interest in a literary work.[2] But the fact remains that within or beneath all the fine shades, two fundamentally contrasting operations are going on. That Paul's book was 'important' functions as identity element to the assertion that he is 'wonderfully on the right road', but that St George was 'inexpressibly droll' when he said it was important functions as inverse element to both.

2. This point is resumed in chapter 6, p. 101 below.

Nuance aside, these two contrasting fundamental operations would make possible a systematic discrimination of further series of items, or 'layers', in a narrative.

V

Conceptions of 'fable' and 'subject' will not fit the threefold division which thus emerges. Perhaps the three fundamentally distinct kinds of items which have been distinguished might be termed: *presented* items, *progressive* items and *density* items. The first are the episodes of narration (or, largely, of description) by the author, or more particularly of conversation among the characters, which make up the actual bulk of the fiction in the sequence in which it comes to the reader. Certain items function as inverse elements *vis-à-vis* these episodes and cancel them as such; but not everything within them. What is not so cancelled is thereby established as constituting another part of the organization of the fiction.

A second part of the organization may be seen as the progressive items (the 'B series' above), progressive in that they are the stages between the initial state of affairs in the narrative and the final state. This series of items may include inverse elements (that is particularly common, for example, in folk-tales where the hero succeeds only at the third attempt or the like) and then the series of events between the initial and final states might be said to contain recursive loops; but it cannot include any identity elements. This is what is meant by the word 'progressive': such an element would by definition simply not be a 'stage' at all. Identity elements must therefore be classified as a third part of the organization, the arrayed series of the 'density' items. A density item cannot be an inverse item, and must be an identity item, *vis-à-vis* the progressive items (the 'B series'). Whether or not the first Mrs St George was 'one of the really great administrators and disciplinarians' (p. 152), she dies: and whether or not Marian was 'an artistic intelligence really of the first order', Paul falls in love with her and St George marries her.

It might be thought that more could be said of the progressive items than, rather negatively, has been said so far: for example, that they may be arranged in non-interchangeable temporal series. But it seems that this is sometimes true and sometimes not. Often enough, the series of the progressive items is a sparse one. In *A Boring Story* there seem, as we saw, to be only three unreversed events which make up the difference between the initial and the closing situations and so may be said to belong to the progressive series:

B_1 – Nikolai goes to Karkhov
B_2 – Lisa and Gnekker get secretly married
B_3 – Nikolai approaches his own death (suggested not explicit)

In *Love Among the Haystacks* there are perhaps also only three events of this kind:

B_1 – Geoffrey is united to Lydia (she does not leave her husband save inasmuch as this takes place)
B_2 – Maurice is united to Paula
B_3 – Geoffrey and Maurice are reconciled

We may now ask an important question. What formal relations, other than inverse or identity functions, exist among the progressive items? Formal relations such as parallelism, contrast, equivalence or identity, augmentation, diminution, opposition, and so on, are common and prominent among the progressive items in much fiction. Let us ask what relations of this kind may be found among the progressive items in narratives such as we are now considering. The answer is a remarkable one: we have to answer that in fiction like this, such relations are rudimentary or (as in *A Boring Story*) almost non-existent.

With regard to the density-items in this kind of fiction, however, that is very much not the case; in fact, one could perhaps begin to characterize this whole kind of fiction by saying that it displays a massive transference of formal relationships away from the progressive items, and on to the density-items. The relationship of equality or equivalence is obviously very common. St George is 'the Master', in various formulations, almost throughout. Then there are the relations of opposition, both as between one character, say, and another, and as between the temporal stages of the narrative, Paul is merely a 'young aspirant' at the beginning, but his new novel is spoken of, at least, as 'really magnificent' at the end. Much also is done, throughout any density series, to sustain an awareness in the reader not simply of contrast and cancellation, but of certain continuous processes. These are not at all processes of actual change in the situation of the fiction – such would belong among the progressive items, the series B – but they may be processes of progressive *revelation* of the state of affairs. In *The Lesson of the Master* the 'young aspirant' of the beginning has, even then, also a 'degree of identity' (p. 116); long before the crucial phase of the narrative from the point of view of its progressive series, he is declared to be 'wonderfully on the right road' (p. 153). All these items in the multiplicity of 'density-series' contribute to the creation of a network of formal relationships which inter-connect the narrative as a whole. Paul's apparent stature at the beginning proves to *contrast* with that which he is seen to have at the end, and likewise with St George; on the other hand, each at the start is to some extent the *equivalent* of the other at the close (though of course the novelist whose 'vein' is 'exhausted' is also a contrast to the 'young aspirant': but yet again, is the re-married St George an aspirant after all once again?). Likewise Marian and Mrs St George. They *resemble*, throughout, in their feminine attractiveness and suitability in that respect as a wife; but each is also revealed as in other respects the *opposite* of the other (though of course, the deeper layers of James's irony call this in its turn into question, and invite us to see the two women as perhaps essentially alike in spite of all).

In identifying such formal structures in the arrays of density items, only a very few out of a mass of details can be specifically mentioned. Another revealing case is that of Lydia in *Love Among the Haystacks*. There is both continuity and contrast in how she is presented. On the one hand:

> Her face was . . . comely . . . she gave an impression of cleanness . . . she would have been pretty (p. 24)
>
> she looked little more than a girl . . . small, and natty, with neat little features (p. 36)
>
> she was fresh from washing, and looked very pretty . . . neat and pretty, with a sweet womanly gravity (p. 46)

But alongside these there are quite other ideas.

> comely, save for the look of bitterness and aloofness (p. 24)
>
> 'Don't you bother about me', she remonstrated, almost irritably (p. 37)
>
> She sounded very determined, even vindictive (p. 39)

With Paula there is a similar but contrary pattern, created with much economy:

> Bits of hay stuck in her hair, and she was white faced. . . Paula understood, and was silent . . . 'you cold?' asked Paula tenderly (p. 46)

It is clear that when 'she went to live at the farm' at the close of the story, another side of her came to the fore, and there were not going to be the same troubles as when she lived at the Vicarage. In all, the opening and closing items in the series stand in a clear inter-relation.

But if inter-relations like this one are clear, they are also, easily enough, made complex and elaborate. They provide opportunities, that is, for the formal relations within the narrative as a whole to be much more definite and much more elaborate than they otherwise would be. Items which we have called 'progressive' items can have formal relations one to another only to a limited extent. Perhaps, indeed, they can sustain only a relation of logical contradiction or its absence (*not both* 'St. George marries Marian' and 'Paul marries Marian'). But the density-items can introduce formal relations of a number of kinds, and the author may multiply and complicate them as much as he wishes. No one could be more distinguished academically than Nikolai, but by the end of the narrative we have come to see that no one's life could be emptier. That is not all. For Nikolai there is an outer emptiness and also an equivalent emptiness within himself. This is not all either, because paradoxically, the inner emptiness of his life goes with a clear comprehension of that, and a sense of what it would be like to be the opposite. In *Love Among the Haystacks*, Geoffrey and Maurice both begin full of enmity and also loneliness. They are opposite extremes. At the end reconciliation contrasts with enmity, and togetherness with isolation, while on the other hand there is a likeness between them instead of a contrast. All the time, and in many ways, one can see the density-items creating relations of contrariety or inversion, extreme and counter-extreme, or change from minimum to maximum or from incipience to culmination.

Likeness and sameness, whether overt or implicit, is important. Part of *Love Among the Haystacks* is that release or fulfilment for Maurice, to whom life comes easily, is much like what it is for Geoffrey to whom life comes hard. Marian and the first Mrs St George may contrast as potential wives for a creative artist, but there is also quite another line of development in the book. One example of this is the passage where Marian says to Paul 'I liked your book', when he has written not one but three or four books. Another is how she says goodbye to him 'in her young purity and richness . . . almost ashamed of that exercise of the pen which it

was her present *inclination* to commend'. Again St George's creative powers as a 'fine *original* source' are mentioned almost immediately after we hear of the *something so fresh and sound in the
originality* of the large smooth house' (p. 110). Ultimately, the text
suggests, St George's creativity is equivalent of that of the (long-
dead) fashionable architect, mere clever servant of the quality.
The Russian text of *A Boring Story* likewise establishes a crucial
identity between Nikolai's seeming-prim and conventional
daughter, and his wayward, loose-living ward. Lisa says, 'I don't
know, how everything can be so *burdensome* to me ('Ya ne znayu,
chto so mnoyu . . . tyazhelo!'); and on the very next page Katya
echoes this with 'ah, if you were to know how *burdensome* life is to
me' ('Akh, esli b vȳ znali, kak mne bȳlo tyazhelo!'). The Penguin
translation does not reproduce this equivalence, and so conceals,
at this particular point, how Nikolai's world has only one and the
same thing to offer to all, however seemingly different from one
another they may be.

Perhaps it is in the nature of things that the progressive items in
a narrative, the 'events' in a straightforward sense, cannot often be
rich in contrasts. Contrasting events can of course sometimes
occur, but the common case is perhaps simply that either the
event occurs, or it does not. Also, many events do not admit of
degree. Relations such as contrareity, minimum to maximum,
incipience to culmination, possibility to self-evident certainty, do
not readily arise in respect of them. Hence it is the density items
which above all give not only 'density of specification' in James's
words, but that ordered and patterned density of specification
which is the major part of the structure of the narrative.

No doubt such formal patterns may constitute an autonomous
part of the fiction and create a self-dependent stimulus and pleasure within the experience of reading it. There is much in James's
later critical writing that shows he had this side of things largely in
view. But that is not the whole of the matter. In such fiction as
these three tales, the density-items may be seen in the end *to group
themselves around certain general conceptions*. In *A Boring Story*, we
have on the one hand the idea that Nikolai identifies, towards the
end, as the great lack within himself: '. . . what is known as a
ruling idea, or what might be termed the god of the living man
. . . and if that is not there, nothing is there' (p. 101). In *The Lesson
of the Master*, there is the 'decent perfection' (p. 153) of art pursued
with dedication, as against, 'the full rich masculine human general

life' (p. 158) and its feminine counterpart in Marian's 'young purity and richness' (p. 120); as also the web of social protocol and acquisitiveness that we glimpse as the background and foundation of the tale, and are reminded of when once, casually, naively, Marian identifies 'London' and 'life' (p. 140). In *Love Among the Haystacks* there are the twin conceptions of a 'hardening' of the personality and of when it is 'softened again' into 'spring' and 'release' (p. 40).

In respect of those three tales, such remarks of course represent only a beginning. But it seems that, in presenting and manipulating the general conceptions with which the events of his tale are associated, a writer does, above all, two things. First, we may say that he *asseverates* the importance of the conceptions that are involved. They mean, he implies, so exceedingly much; their full significance cannot come out in one; they have to be rehearsed over and over. The very words for them are packed with density of meaning:

> 'What I mean is have you it in your heart to go in for some sort of decent perfection?'
> 'Ah decency, ah perfection – !' the young man sincerely sighed.

That is a scrap of very clear and pure asseveration, put by James into the dialogue of the characters. Such a conception, it is implied, invites and requires a great amount of deepening, to be done over the whole length of the fiction. It emerges slowly into view: or rather, what emerges is its full weight and magnitude, its inescapability and irreplaceability. These are the aspects of it that asseveration serves.

Second, the writer *polarizes* his conceptions. He uses the length and elaboration of his work to bring out, more and more clearly and inescapably, that between one conception and another there is a total and final opposition. This is what St George has to say to Paul about perfection on the one hand, and the 'rich general life' on the other. For Chekhov, 'if that is not there, nothing is there': between real fulfilment and life, and mere conventional eminence, there is no compromise, no half-and-half position. Between the qualities of life potential in Lydia, and all the potential, such as it was, of her first husband, there was total opposition, life against death.

It may be said that asseveration, on the whole, occurs through more or less consecutive items in the same density series. Polarization occurs rather between one series and another, or between the beginning of a series and the end. But in all these cases, associating the narrative with general conceptions has the effect of enriching the patterns of formal relations among the arrays of items making up the density series; and so the patterning and structuring of the narrative as a whole. What happens in the kind of fiction which has been discussed, is that there is a massive shift in the formal relationships, in the patterning and so the structure, from the progressive series, to the whole collection of series of density items. By means of the ideas of inverse and identity elements, applied in a general way to narrative series, it is possible to distinguish the presented items, the progressive items and the density items more systematically than would otherwise be so; and therefore, to identify and observe that shift.

One final point is worth making if only as a suggestion. To the degree that a narrative takes the form, not of a series of progressive items directly presented or at least directly narrated, but of a series of dialogue episodes, or of narrated episodes which terminate with inverse elements, and through which such progressive items as the narrative contains emerge into the reader's consciousness indirectly and perhaps inconspicuously – to the degree that a narrative takes that form, a very distinctive consequence ensues. This is, that the series of the progressive items (the 'story' in the plain old-fashioned sense) – recedes into the background. The very means whereby it is transmitted at all seem to tell the reader that the main interest is not there. Where then is it? Not, self-evidently, in the mere fact that the characters talk: if only, because that is repeatedly cancelled by the inverse items. It must therefore be in what they say or think, or what is said about them as they talk. In other words, the Jamesian method of narration by 'scenes' (Chekhov's and Lawrence's method here too) of its own nature throws the stress off the 'plot' and on to the density items, where the form and structure prove in the main to be. Characters who talk are characters with ideas in a fiction of ideas.

Chekhov, A., *A Boring Story* in *Lady with Lapdog and other stories* (Penguin, 1964), pp. 46–104.

Lawrence, D. H., *Love Among the Haystacks* in *Love Among the Haystacks and other stories* (Penguin, 1960), pp. 7–48.

James, H., 'The Lesson of the Master', *Selected Tales of Henry James* (Richards Press, London 1947), pp. 109–76.

5

Narrative structure and text structure: Isherwood's *A Meeting by the River* and Muriel Spark's *The Prime of Miss Jean Brodie*

I

It may add to the lucidity of this chapter (and I doubt that its *drama* will be much impaired) if I summarize in advance what each of its sections will attempt. Section II argues that a narrative consists of a set of 'runs' of events; considers certain preliminary ways in which the narrative interrelates the 'runs'; argues that some operation or operations may be seen as defining the passage from one event in a run to another; and analyses *A Meeting by the River* so as to suggest that, in this particular case, the operations required may be seen as a significant part of the narrative structure. Section III argues that a quite different narrative operation plays much the same role in the structure of Muriel Spark's novel. Section IV discusses the part played in narrative structure by what is here called (barbarously) 'causalization': that is to say, what the writer does as he works causal interrelations (doubtless implicit) into every part of the runs referred to in section II. Finally, section V sketches (in respect to Miss Spark's novel only) a few of the further processes which seem to underlie the difference between the rudimentary set of runs (as these may be imagined, needless to say) and the final full text of a narrative, with all its incidental detail; and argues that this difference also may be considered from the point of view of structure. It may be added that I selected the two novels because I had to reread them for other purposes, do not suppose that they are especially amenable to the present approach to narrative structure, and therefore hope that they may be illustrative of what has wider interest or application. The present discussion does not claim that its use of the term 'structure' in respect of narrative is the only possible sense, or even the most important one.

II

Any narrative may be considered as a set of items, whether characters, initial facts about them or their setting, or events that happen to them. This is true, even though occasionally there may be doubt as to whether a certain postulated event is or is not part of that narrative: as we know that Goneril's marriage to Albany is one of the facts about the work *King Lear* and Goneril's marriage to Cornwall is not, but do not really know (in my view) what to say about the postulated event 'Goneril's falling in love with Edmund', because it is no part of Shakespeare's purpose to indicate whether or not this is the right description of what she did.

If (this peripheral difficulty aside) we think of a narrative as a set, or set of sets, then by the structure of the narrative we mean something about the relations between members of this set or sets, or about relations between such relations. The more we know about such matters the more we know about the structure, or the more elaborate we think the structure is. The material of the work is complex, but there are more or less simple, and more or less all-inclusive, relation patterns which may be said to be implicit within it. Identifying them means identifying structure. This is therefore a reductive activity; but to suggest, as is sometimes done, that every reductive statement obscures matters more important than those it elucidates is itself a reductive statement.

Some recent discussions of narrative structure consider the narrative as a sequence of events, and assume that the structure is what is manifested by the relation between any given event and the event $(n - 1)$,[1] or perhaps the whole sequence from the first event up to the $(n - 1)$th event in the book. In the present discussion this approach will be modified in two ways. It will be modified, later on, by considering what would be happening if the writer were revising his work into the final version, out of a penultimate version which was, as it were, a next-most-complex version: one to which some final 'complexifying' process has not yet been applied. The other way in which the present discussion will modify that approach is that it will consider narrative not as one sequence of events but as an interrelated set of sequences.

This may be shown to be a necessary postulate in respect of

1. E.g. R. Barthes, 'Introduction à l'analyse structurale du récit', *Communications*, no. 8 (1966), pp. 1–27.

most works of classic Western European fiction. It may of course always be determined which of two events occurred first in the sequence of the *narration*. To say so is only to say that if a and b are words in a text, and R the relation of 'occurring before', then aRb or bRa. This is not the same, though, as the sequence of events as it is intended that the reader should understand them as having occurred in the tale that the narrative narrates – the *narrated*. Thus (to cite *King Lear* again), the text has Goneril kissing Edmund before it mentions the King of France's having left his army at Dover in order to return to his own country. Whether the author intended us to infer that the events occurred in that same order, or the reverse order, cannot be decided. There is not either the one order of events or the other. There is no order as between them. The work simply does not contain any sequence within which these two events are successive. Nothing is lost, thereby, in this particular case.

This example makes clear how a literary narrative need not be a single sequence of events: on the contrary, most literary narratives are complexes consisting of several sequences. By definition, the sequential relations between the items in each run are determined exhaustively; but the sequential relations between items in the various runs may not be so. Such a narrative work is therefore like a partially ordered set in the mathematical sense; and many literary works may, from the narrative point of view, be illustrated at least up to a point by what are called Hasse diagrams. More of this later.

The events narrated in Isherwood's *A Meeting by the River* (henceforth Σ_1) are few in number. Even so, the total set of events may be divided up into at least three runs, and I believe that all readers of the novel would admit that relations of sequence could not be established as between certain items in two or more different runs (this fact, indeed, is what determines the number of runs, though in practice readers would probably use other and less rigorous methods).

The three runs, or sequences of events, may be summarized as follows:

> (a) *The tale of Oliver.* An acolyte at a Hindu monastery is about to become a full monk, but under the influence of his brother he nearly abandons this design and nearly becomes the lover of his brother's wife. Then the brother's influence ceases and he becomes a monk after all.

(b) *The tale of Patrick*. A married man is thrown off balance by an affair with a younger person, so that under the influence of his brother he nearly becomes a Hindu monk: but the influence ceases and he remains a married man after all.

(c) *The tale of Tom*. A young person becomes the lover of an older one and is about to join him in a distant part of the world; but the influence ceases and he reverts to his original situation.

The next point is an important one: the individual runs may be combined into a single narrative by straightforward 'embedding' operations: transformations in the linguist's sense. We attach to the words 'his brother' in (a), a relative clause of which the *NP* (subject) is 'the married man thrown off balance' in (b); and to this, another relative clause with something like 'the older man of whom the young person becomes the lover' from (c). Correspondingly throughout, in fact. The resulting sentence would be tediously complex and cumbrous, but that does not affect the issue of principle. The point is that the embedding transformations could carry out the interrelating systematically and completely. If so, they represent the structure. We could therefore say that $\Sigma_1 = f(a,b,c)$, where f is a function, in something rather like the formal logic or mathematical sense, denoting the total of embedding transformations which may be systematically performed as above. In practice, these results are achieved by the use of proper names: we rewrite 'Oliver' for 'an acolyte' in *a* and for 'his brother' in *b*. We rewrite 'Patrick' for 'his brother' in *a*, 'a married man' in *b*, and 'an older man' in *c*. We rewrite 'Tom' for 'a young person' in *b* and *c* as well.

There is a tale also of Penelope, Patrick's wife. It is rather a minimal tale (Penelope does not write any letters in this epistolary novel), but it is worth while to summarize how it might run:

(d) *The tale of Penelope*. A certain married woman was nearly deserted by her husband, who fell under the influence of a young person; but the influence ceases and the situation reverts to what it was before.

That formulation, however, is not altogether satisfactory, because the first part of the sentence only says, over again, what Patrick nearly did. We have in fact no idea of what Penelope nearly did. The most we can say is something like 'her situation was nearly transformed'. Is this not a clue, however? The expression 'her situation was nearly transformed' is a much more general one than what appeared at the corresponding points in the three runs set out previously. Yet this is to notice that there are 'corresponding points' in all the four runs. Suppose we now try to rewrite the other runs, rewrite them downward and backward, as it were, into the most generalized and rudimentary forms we can find. Beginning with *a*, we should get something like:

> (*a*) A character *A* is in a certain situation of attachment to someone or something else, but under the influence of someone outside his situation he nearly moves into a situation the opposite of his first situation. Then the influence ceases and the character reverts to his original situation.

Certainly that formulation is very generalized (and of course boring); but it is not a vacuous or tautological formulation. It does not by any means describe what happens to any character in any work whatsoever, nor even any large and obvious class of characters; but it does describe what happens to Oliver in Σ_1. More than that, it describes equally well what happened to Patrick, to Tom, and to Penelope. It is worth noting, in extension of this, that every situation in the novel is one either of attachment and devotion (to a wife, a brother, or a monastery and its way of life), or else is the cancelling of such an attachment and the establishing of a contrary state of affairs. Here it is important to note that the distinction is not one simply of a '*p*/ not *p*' kind. It is much more specific than that. Distinctions like 'lover of a married woman/Hindu monk', or 'happily married husband/homosexual lover', we may briefly say, represent something like *opposite poles of experience*. In relating the narrative structure to these distinctions, therefore, we shall not be engaging in an empty and tautological operation.[2]

If so, more may be said about structure in Σ_1; or if you like one may say that it has more structure, or a more fully determined structure, than has appeared so far or than was suggested by the runs *a, b, c, d* above. What now transpires is this: given that the items in each of the four runs, and the relations between them, are characterized in sufficiently general terms, then the items, and more particularly the relations between them, *turn out to be the same in every case*. This may be put another way. The relation between any item in a sequence and its successor is defined by the

---

2. Prof. Steiner has drawn my attention to the importance of this point, as also to the clarifications attempted on pp. 90–1 below.

operation or operations which must be performed in order to arrive at the second item from the first. To think about the relation, and to think about the operations which must be performed, are two ways of thinking about the same thing. Therefore, in respect of Σ_1, we may say that the same operations are to be performed throughout each of the four runs which constitute the total narrative, in order to reach the successive items in the runs. In fact, in Σ_1 the runs are unusually short and simple. They may be considered as having an initial item, a middle item, and a final one (the general problems raised by elaboration beyond this minimum are touched on below, in section v). But in each case, the middle item is to be reached by performing the same operation on the initial item.

This operation might be expressed as '*nearly* convert the initial item into a contrary item'. Patrick nearly becomes a monk, Tom nearly becomes Patrick's permanent lover, Oliver nearly becomes Penelope's lover (which he was, we understand, long before the novel opened), Penelope nearly becomes a deserted woman. It may be noted once again that in each case the operation is not to produce merely the *contradictory* of the existing state of affairs (i.e., to deny or negate it) but to produce a specific *contrary* of it; and of course the word 'nearly', in the account of that operation, was also important.[3] Isherwood could very well have written a novel in which Oliver did indeed revert to being Penelope's lover or Patrick the established and permanent lover of Tom (or a Hindu monk, or both for all I know); and correspondingly with the others in each case. But it would have been a different novel, precisely in that the middle items would have been reached from the initial ones by an operation other than what we have.

The terminal item in each of the four runs is also to be obtained, in the particular case of Σ_1, by a single operation, one the same in the case of each of them. This operation is a significant one and may be described as that of *de-transformation*. It is not uncommonly to be found at one stage or another in literary works, and especially perhaps at the end of them. The operation amounts simply to reversing a previous operation, whatever that may

3. It should be noted that the operation given as 'near contrarize' is not 'bring about a nearly contrary state', but '*nearly* bring about the contrary state' (the distinction here between 'a' and 'the' is significant, of course).

happen to have been. The case of Patrick is anomalous and inter-esting, and I do not quite know how it should be treated. We may say that the contrarizing operation is performed twice over in the story: once to obtain the item that he nearly became the perma-nent lover of Tom, and once again to obtain the item that he nearly became a Hindu monk. So, the de-transforming operation must also be performed twice over in order to obtain, as the final item in the string, the initial item over again. Since the two events occur very largely (though not, it must be admitted, altogether) independently of each other and without influence on each other, we could perhaps consider that two separate tales were told in respect of Patrick; and represent his position in the novel by two runs instead of one. This is a simplification of the book. Without it, the analysis in terms of 'near contrarization' and subsequent de-transformation I think remains valid, but it is more difficult to express in straightforward but also general terms. If we adopt the simplification, we could represent the runs in the novel and the operations consecutively performed upon them in a diagram (see figure 2).

Some may find it helpful to consider the operations as succes-sive functions of a variable x of which a, b_1, b_2, c, and d are individual values, as in algebra or formal logic; but there is no need to do so, and I have indicated the successive operations verbally. The diagram as a whole looks like an aggregate of *Hasse diagrams*.[4] We must, however, be clear that the element of struc-ture identified so far is in no way represented by the pattern of *lines* collectively considered: it is represented by the *continuity* of the lines and by the *identity of the operations* which are to be performed, in each case, at corresponding points along them. To emphasize how in each case the final state is the same as the initial one, the diagrams could be drawn on the surface of a cylinder with time represented by a determinate direction around the cylinder. Possibly this is better, because it represents the time of the novel as bounded, and it makes good sense to say that there is no novel time before the beginning of the book or after the end of it (see figure 3).

4. A Hasse diagram is an oriented scheme of points and connecting lines used to picture a partially ordered set, i.e., to suggest visually which elements of the set bear a certain relation to which other elements of the set.

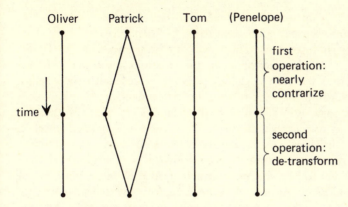

Figure 2. Narrative operations in $\Sigma 1$.

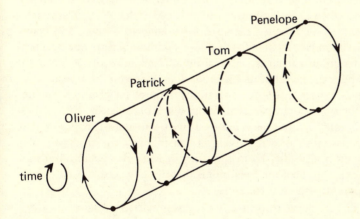

Figure 3. Cyclic form of figure 2.

III

Muriel Spark's *The Prime of Miss Jean Brodie* (henceforth referred to as Σ_2) is more intricate than Σ_1. First, it has more characters: Miss Brodie the schoolmistress, Miss Mackay the headmistress, Teddy Lloyd the art master, Gordon Lowther the music master, Miss Lockhart the science mistress, several minor adult characters, and a number of schoolgirls one of whom is of major importance. I am inclined to represent the narrative of this novel by seven runs, each relating to a different character. It must be noted also that in the course of the whole novel Miss Brodie herself is intricately involved in several quite separable areas of activity. We see her relations to her 'set' of pupils ('set' is used here in the snob sense, as in the novel), to the headmistress, to Teddy, to Gordon. Beyond this again, the situations in which the characters find themselves cannot possibly be reduced to any single relationship (like the relation of 'attachment' in Σ_1) or its contradictory. We at least have the relations of 'employs', 'teaches lessons to', 'loves', 'sleeps with' (in the usual meiosis sense), as substantial relations, not further reducible between characters; and others, also, surely, relations such as 'is a friend to', 'chooses for lover to . . .', or 'represents in a picture'. Here, perhaps, we should glance back at Σ_1. Of course, it is true that to reduce the relations in that narrative between one character and another to the single relations of 'is attached to' (with its contradictory) largely emptied that novel of its content and impoverished it *pro tanto*. Every reader knows, for example, that Patrick's attachments to his brother, his wife, his young male lover, and (for a brief moment) to the life of religious withdrawal are qualitatively different in each case. But although the substitution partially empties the novel of its *content*, it does not reduce to nonsense its *structure*. The successive operations required to 'produce' the line of the story can be performed. But if we try to reduce the relations in Σ_2 still further, this is not so. If we try to assimilate 'loves' and 'sleeps with', it is impossible to distinguish the story of Miss Brodie and Teddy from the story of Miss Brodie and Gordon, whereas in the book the point is that these two stories are indeed different: and so throughout.

The narrative runs in Σ_2 will be summarized in more abridged form than those in Σ_1 (Σ_2 is a novel with more by way of incidental event). Moreover, not all of them are full-length runs: several, that is to say, effectively begin subsequent to the opening of what was called, earlier on, the *narrated*, or effectively terminate after its close (they cannot of course do either of these things in respect of the narration). I should perhaps add that several of the words employed in the run summaries (e.g., 'wrong', 'teach', 'betray') must be taken with reserve. They may be said to be valid within the surface conventions of Σ_2, but the novel, in using them, draws attention to the fact that their use has become conventionalized to the point of emptiness. It seems to me that Σ_2 draws attention to this but does not make it its business to labour at redefining such terms as 'teach' or (sexual) 'wrong'.

Some will think the omission grave: others, including myself, not.

Here are the run summaries which I propose for Σ_2:

> (*a*) A teacher is employed to teach a class of girls their lessons, but she does not effectively teach them any lessons. (She may teach them other things.)

> (*b*) A headmistress *hopes* to dismiss one of her assistants for any of various reasons but does so in the end for a reason quite other than all of them.

> (*c*) A woman loves a man and he her, but she does not sleep with him.

> (*d*) A painter sleeps with one woman all the time (this is his wife) and with others from time to time; but he keeps on representing in his pictures a woman he does not sleep with.

> (*e*) A woman sleeps with a man but does not love him nor he her; she *believes* she can marry him but he suddenly marries elsewhere.

> (*f*) A woman loves a man but *promotes* one of her protegées to sleep with him; this protegée does not do so, but another protegée does.

> (*g*) A woman chooses one of her protegées to be her special confidante, but is betrayed by her.

> (*h*) A teacher continually does a wrong thing but is not dismissed for it; but is dismissed for something she did not do. (Miss Brodie doesn't teach the children anything at all in a formal sense, let alone 'teach Fascism'.)

> (*i*) A schoolgirl is specially *trusted* by a teacher but betrays her. Later she becomes a nun but remains un–nunlike.

> (*j*) A teacher lives a very quiet and business-like life, but she suddenly marries a man who has long had a mistress.

An integrated summary of the novel in this case also may be constructed by embedding operations on the individual runs ('a woman who is a teacher who . . .', 'one of her assistants who loves a man who all the time sleeps with . . .', etc., etc.). In this context it may be observed that in some cases more than one of the run summaries above in fact denote the same train of events. Thus *b* is as it were the mirror image of *h*, *g* is mirror image of the first part of *i*. The embedding may of course be done by inserting the characters' names: for 'a man' in *c*, 'a painter' in *d*, and 'a man' in *f*, we may rewrite 'Teddy Lloyd' every time; for 'another protegée' in f, 'one of her protegées' in g, and 'a schoolgirl' in i, we may rewrite 'Sandy' every time; and so throughout.

It is clear that the operations required to 'produce' the various runs ('produce' is being used in something like a geometrical sense) cannot be assimilated in Σ_2 as they could be in Σ_1. All the same, there is one pervasive feature which is structural because once again it comprises the crucial operation by means of which the later items in the runs may be obtained from the earlier. This pervasive structural feature is drawn attention to by a syntactical feature in the run summaries above: the recurrence of the conjunction 'but' conjoining an earlier item to a later one.

That at least is the case, if 'but' really does indicate a single constant operation which has to occur each time the word appears. What could such an operation be? There is a clue in the words italicized in the catalogue of runs summarized above. These surely bring out that Σ_2 (like a very large proportion of literary works) operates not through the medium of sequences of actual events alone but also (or probably 'but rather . . .') through interactions between events, on the one hand, and such things as expectations, hopes, or fears, on the other. In part, the presence and the importance of expectations, hopes, or fears is made quite explicit in the runs by words such as 'hopes' in b, 'believes' in e, 'promotes' (i.e., puts forward in the hope that) in f, and 'is trusted by' (i.e., expected to help, not hinder) in i. But there is more to the point than this.

There are certain expectations, hopes, or fears which a reader readily brings to his reading of a novel, or more strictly (in the case of hopes and fears anyway) readily ascribes to the characters in the novel, without the novelist's having to insist on them. The reader does so through a combination of inductive generalizations about human behaviour, on the one hand, and conventions established for fiction, or at least for traditional Western fiction, on the other. Thus, to say that A loves B entitles the reader to expect that A will hope to marry or to sleep with B. Similarly, for a teacher continually to do a 'wrong' thing creates (certainly within the conventions relevant to Edinburgh girls' schools in the 1930s) expectation that he or she will be dismissed for it; or that she is 'employed to teach', an expectation that she will do so. If A chooses B as confidante, that creates an expectation that B will not betray A.

These expectations are not immutable. In fact, once they have been surprised and disappointed often enough by the narrative, the very act on the writer's part of creating a conventional pattern of expectation will be sufficient to make the reader expect something else as the outcome in fact. One may cite as analogy (it is nothing more) the significances of the first and second differential coefficients of an equation. The first differential coefficient indicates the slope of the curve of the equation; and we may say that it can create certain legitimate expectations as to future values of the curve. But if the second differential (which indicates not how the curve but how the steepness of the curve is changing) is negative when the first differential is positive, expectations about further values will be reversed. By the time the reader gets to the later pages of Σ_2, he will probably have carried out something like a second differentiation and will be expecting Miss Brodie to be dismissed for anything rather than for her *amours*.

It would be useful to have a single word for expectations *or* hopes *or* fears. One possibility is the word 'forward' as in forward buying and so on. A distinction may be drawn between such forwards on the part of the reader and on the part of a character in the narrative; but it is not fundamental. Every forward on a character's part may be re-stated as a related forward on the reader's part: often an expectation instead of a hope or fear, sometimes a part-for-whole relation or the reverse, occasionally a contradictory.

We can now state the crucial operation which 'produces' the narrative runs in Σ_2. It is something like: 'If there exists a forward in respect of a given situation or event, write the subsequent event so as to negate that forward.' This is the operation, we may say, which regularly produces the nth event in Σ_2 from the $(n-1)$th. More strictly, we ought perhaps to speak of something like a *'primary* forward': because (as I said) by the closing pages of the book the reader is not forming expectations as he did at the beginning but has become aware of the pattern of the narrative and has begun to make a routine of expecting the opposite of the expected. The fact remains that the structure of this narrative is largely a matter of the constant operation of writing a next event so as to negate an existing forward. This may be compared to a switching device such that when one acts so as to complete a certain circuit, the circuit is in fact broken, and an alternative circuit is completed instead. I shall not pursue this point, but it means that the kind of structure we are here identifying is characteristic of complexes in a number of widely differing fields.

We may now, bearing in mind how certain of the summaries were mirror images of each other or of parts of each other, represent the narrative in Σ_2, for the moment, by the reduced number of *six* lattice chains (two of them almost minimal ones) for the characters of Miss Mackay, Miss Brodie, Sandy, Teddy, Gordon, and Miss Lockhart. I represent this first in simplified form, without linkages between the runs, in order to show the ubiquitousness of the 'switching device'; this being the actual uniformity of structure in the narrative. The events which occur at the switch points are listed below (see the numbering in figure 4). It should be noted that some of these are reiterated events – they take place again and again – and as such become almost part of the standing conditions of the situation toward the middle of the story. Time, as before for Σ_1, is represented by an axis running from the top of the diagram to the bottom.

1. Miss Mackay employs Miss Brodie but doesn't wish to.

2. Miss Brodie is employed to teach Sandy, Rose, etc., their 'lessons' but doesn't.

3. Miss Brodie loves Teddy but doesn't sleep with him.

4. Miss Brodie sleeps with Gordon but doesn't love him.

5. Miss Mackay hopes to dismiss Miss Brodie for her *amours* but can't.

6. Teddy paints a picture of Rose, but it turns out like Miss Brodie.

7. Gordon sleeps with Miss Brodie but suddenly marries Miss Lockhart.

8. Miss Lockhart is a quiet, unsexy person but suddenly marries a rather 'fast' man.

9. Miss Brodie still loves Teddy but promotes Rose to sleep with him.

10. Miss Brodie chooses Sandy as confidante, but Sandy dislikes her.

11. Sandy is chosen as confidante but sleeps with Teddy.

12. Teddy paints a picture of Sandy, but it too turns out like Miss Brodie.

13. Sandy is still chosen as confidante, but she betrays Miss Brodie.

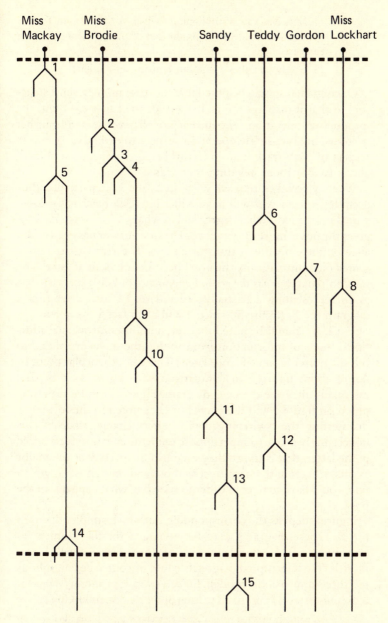

Figure 4. Occurrences in Σ_2 of the 'switching' operation (= negate an existing forward) in respect of six major narrative runs (compare figure 5).

14. Miss Mackay is still hoping to dismiss Miss Brodie for her amours but suddenly finds she can dismiss her for 'teaching Fascism'.

15. Sandy becomes a nun but remains un–nunlike.

Once again it should be noted that the diagram represents structure in that it displays the recurrence of the run–extending, the 'productive' operation. The runs do not all have the same number of items, but one single operation suffices to extend *every* run in respect of *every* fresh item in it: this being the operation defined above (p. 85) about negating forwards.

We may now begin to ask what, in Σ_1 and Σ_2 in particular (but doubtless the answer will have wider interest), *connects* the individual runs; and to what degree and in what ways this connecting gives the novel more of structure. The first answer has been given already: the embedding transformations. If these also are represented diagrammatically the point becomes obvious at once. The resulting diagram *has the general appearance* of being a Hasse diagram representing a partially ordered set.[5] I shall offer first a diagram for Σ_2 (figure 5), since it will be in fact a completion of figure 4. (It should be noted that certain non–controversial additional items of information from within the novel are added to this diagram for convenience later.) There is a particular point to notice about figure 5 in comparison with figure 4. It is, that essentially they are the *same* diagram. Figure 4 can be superimposed on figure 5 and the events or facts noted in the former as manifesting the 'switching-device' effect characteristic of this novel simply prove to superimpose upon the events or facts noted in the latter: that is to say they establish themselves as the major events or facts in the narrative, as those and only those to which one would have to refer in order to state the 'what happens' of the book.

Figure 6 depicts the corresponding but much simpler diagram for Σ_1. These diagrams may be envisaged for the moment as two-dimensional representations of three-dimensional Hasse models (the interrupted diagonals could of course be continuous in a three-dimensional model). Since a relative pronoun ('who') is to be understood as prefixed to each of the diagonals linking run to

5. 'A partially ordered set is a set of elements x, y, z . . . together with an order relation holding between *some pairs* of elements, and satisfying the reflexive, antisymmetric and transitive laws' (H. G. Flegg, *Boolean Algebra* [London, 1972 ed.], p. 141; my italics).

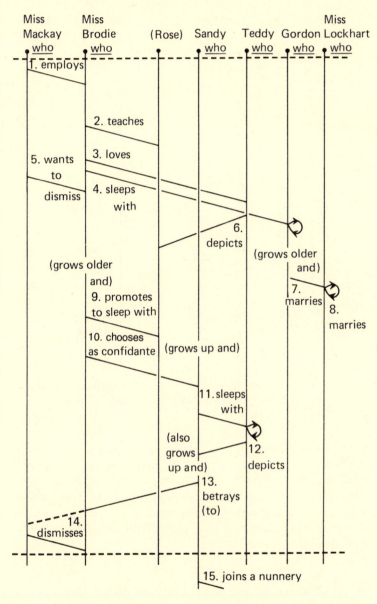

Figure 5. 'Embedding' transformations in Σ_2 integrating the narrative runs. The events described in the embedding clauses are the major events in the narrative and coincide throughout with occurrences of the 'switching' operation (compare figure 4).

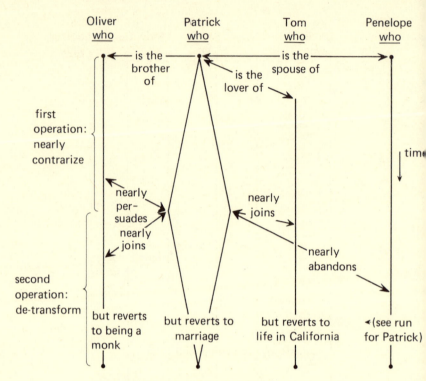

Figure 6. The embedding transformations in Σ_1. Compare figure 2, showing the narrative operations occurring to extend each of the runs.

run, each of the diagrams is also formally equivalent to a (very complex) tree diagram as utilized in linguistics, and in principle, certainly, the events of the narratives Σ_1 and Σ_2 could be summarily recounted in a single complex sentence of which the subject was the central character (or in principle any character), and the doings of other characters were recorded in embedded subordinate clauses.

IV

It was suggested above merely that the two diagrams had *the general appearance* of being Hasse diagrams. On the basis of what had been said so far, they cannot really be considered as such. The lines of a Hasse diagram represent a single constant relation with certain essential formal properties. Those in the diagrams above represent a miscellany of relations: 'employs', 'loves', 'sleeps with', etc. The formal properties of these various relations are not all the same, and in most cases are not those required (see note, p. 88) for structuring a partially ordered set: most of them may be treated as reflexive, but some of them are not antisymmetric (e.g., 'sleeps with' is symmetric, because if A sleeps with B, then B sleeps with A), and few of them are transitive (it is certainly not the case, for example, that 'A loves C' follows from 'A loves B' together with 'B loves C').

Another way of putting the difficulty is to say that, while the diagrams do indeed display the structure of their narratives, insofar as they indicate constancy in the operations performed (this need not be recapitulated), beyond that they are not diagrams of structure but representations merely of the *aggregation* of the work. So far, they represent merely *lists* of events: the main events in the history of each character being listed in a run under his or her name, and the diagonals merely pointing out other runs in which the event in question may also be catalogued.

These diagrams will soon be seen, however, to indicate a further element. At this point the discussion must revert to the 'other way' of considering narrative structure, which was suggested without being developed at the beginning of paragraph 4 of this essay (p. 75); giving attention, that is, to what the writer is involved in doing if he is rewriting his whole piece to its *ultimate* state from its *penultimate* one. If we think of the time axis as running vertically, we could call this 'vertical transformation' – as against horizontal transformation, which is more or less what we have when, at a certain stage in the narration, the writer performs the same operation in several narrative runs (as was particularly clear for Σ_1).

The discussion now begins to work back toward the actual text of the novel: for, of course, the brief summaries with which it has been concerned so far (whether we think of sets of narrative runs, or of the single heavily embedded complex of the summary text), and in which we have been able to encapsulate what of the structure of Σ_1 or Σ_2 has as yet been analysed, are far indeed from the full texts of those works. But is there a certain sense in which one may see the final text of a narrative as in principle the result of a series of generations and transformations, operated successively upon a basic précis such as we have been considering? If the narrative text itself may be seen as such a result, then something important follows: that there is a significant sense in which the *structure* of the narrative text is the *series* of those operations. We should have to think of a number (perhaps a quite small number) of 'horizontal' operations which would generate, and also terminate, the individual runs. Then, once that had been done, there would be 'vertical' generations and transformations, and a large number of them, and certainly more elaborate and lengthy to carry out, which together would give us, in the end, the final full text. Of these 'vertical' transformations the embedding changes would perhaps be the first.[6]

If, with these possibilities in mind, we revert to the basic runs, I think we notice that the expansion by transformation process may perhaps have begun in them even before we thought: for surely in the most basic forms of the narrative strings we should have not 'a woman', 'a headmistress', 'a painter', and so on, but merely 'a person'. If so, one can see the full force of that very early stage of composition which might be called the *naming transformation*: it is, that the names which occur in a novel are not at all like the As and Bs that analysis replaces them by for a moment. Every name carries a sense as well as a denotation. Even at this very preliminary stage we are being given information. The title at least of Σ_2 gives us more information. We know, by the 'Miss' and the surname in the title of Σ_2, that the heroine is in a different position from her pupils; and from the rest of the title we know that she is a woman *in her prime*. It is a lot to know about a woman, and it means a lot in this book. It tells us that Miss Brodie will be growing older – just as Gordon grows older – and that both of them will know it. The characters with Christian names only are (we are told) 'little girls'. But we know that they, at the same time, must be growing up. In fact, there are constant interpolations in the novel about the passage of time ('Miss Brodie was now forty-three'; 'in the late spring of nineteen thirty-three'; 'in the summer of nineteen thirty-five', etc.), and occasional references to the consequences of that. All of these may be seen as the product of later transformations which expand and divagate the basic runs. At the same time, the references merely call up this or that part of what is really the primary postulate in reading a novel belonging to the classic Western tradition in fiction.

What is the upshot of all these indications about status, age, the

6. Cf. T. Todorov. 'Les transformations narratives', in *Poétique de la prose* (Paris, 1971), p. 224.

passage of time? It is something that seems to be a really crucial step in the whole discussion: that by these means and others almost every link in the diagrams, whether from one item in a run to the next consecutive one, or from one run to another, begins to be confirmed as a *causal link*. Many of the links are rendered so implicitly by the points which have just been touched on – the initial information given in the title, characters' names, prefatory material. 'Miss Brodie loves . . . sleeps with . . . *because* she is a woman in her prime.' This is true also, within the conventions of the novel, in regard to the information implicit in the time axis: information which we confidently possess about growing up or growing older in general. Many links of course cannot be given a causal quality from these alone, but they acquire it from their sequential relation to earlier events. Teddy paints a picture of Rose and it turns out to look like Miss Brodie: *because*, he is in love with Miss Brodie. If the reader now looks back at the diagram of either Σ_1 or Σ_2, he will notice a significant fact: the diagonals linking one vertical to another (i.e., one character to another) were inserted into the diagram and became parts of it, simply as a result of the embedding process. They emerged, that is to say, simply as a result of telling the narrative which the work tells, not as an aggregate of unrelated narratives (compare the lists which appear on pp. 76–7, 83), one for each character, but (the result of embedding transformations of members of that aggregate) as a single narrative which interrelates all those characters. However, every linkage[7] which emerged as a result of these embedding transformations *turns out to be a causal linkage*. 'Miss Mackay who *because* she is a headmistress, employs . . . wants to dismiss *because*'; 'Miss Brodie who, *because* she is a woman in her prime, teaches . . . loves . . . sleeps with . . . ; and who *because* she is [the novel implies] a woman rather past her prime,

7. There is at least one element of partial ordering in Σ_2 that is not causal. It has been left aside because its place in this particular novel is very subordinate, but it has had immense structural importance at least in earlier, and especially perhaps in non-Western, fiction. Miss Brodie, we have at one point to add, '*tells the tale* of Hugh who . . .' (her dead wartime lover). It seems that this relation is an independent one and cannot be reduced to a causal relation. This is self-evidently true in many fictional works, and even in the case of Σ_2, if we tried to reduce the tale-telling relation to causal terms ('Miss Brodie . . . *because* Hugh had once loved her,' etc.; or 'because it was her nature to indulge in fantasy . . .' etc.), we should distort the book.

promotes . . . bed-partner for her erstwhile lover'. And so throughout.

This more or less brings the discussion home: for the causal relation is a single constant relation, not a miscellany (compare the point made on p. 91 above), and it is indeed antisymmetric and transitive (and may be regarded as in principle also reflexive). It therefore has the formal properties required for the order relation of a partially ordered set, and its ubiquitous presence in figures 3 and 5 converts them at a stroke into diagrams of partially ordered sets. Every one of the embedded clauses which I referred to earlier can contain a 'therefore'. A constant relation having the necessary formal properties is thus, we may say, superimposed upon the miscellany of relations which is what we had before. The diagram of a partially ordered set is the diagram of a novel having a certain degree of structure. Whether novelists write structured novels because their primary wish is to depict 'reality' or 'experience' and these indeed have structure, or write about experience because they wish to create structured novels and that is a convenient way of doing so, would appear to admit of no simple or general answer; though it admits of local and historical ones.

V

Doubtless novelists never set to work by writing out a set of basic narrative runs, embedding them together, and then expanding to the final text by a series of 'vertical' transformations. That is beside the point. Such a conception of a building up of a novel is not of interest because it describes the actual writing of this or that novel, but because, if it is a valid conception, a description of the process of construction-in-principle becomes a description of the structure of the construction.

One must recognize that the transformations called for are 'optional' in a rather special sense. They may be compared to those involved in rewriting indirect speech as direct (indeed, this could very well be one of them, and often is so). The rules for such re-writing are, to delete 'that', if present, to make certain tense or occasionally other changes, and to insert inverted commas and some expression like 'he said', or 'answered Jim'. But this last rule is not obligatory at any given point, and in this sense is optional. The words may be inserted at any of a number of points, or possibly between any two words in the spoken text. Only, they must be inserted *somewhere*. There are rules like this in mathematics, indeed in arithmetic. In principle, doubtless, a novelist's conception of the structure of his novel could be so articulate, the structure could be so tight, that the rules governing the successive transformations would in the end determine every word and phrase to appear in one position in the final text and no other: but this cannot often be the case in practice.

Somewhat similarly with the successive operations required to convert what (once the embeddings are done) might be called the summary text into a final text. Many operations would be requisite, but few if any at one point in the text and no other. Most obvious, perhaps, are those called for by the chosen literary *form*. Thus the text of Σ_1, as it comes to be expanded and divagated, has sooner or later to be submitted to a transformation which throws it into the form of an epistolary novel. With Σ_2, there would be a transformation which introduced the distinctive *tone*: its note of casual, unintent, ironic detachment. Since the present section is meant to be a brief introduction only, I shall not pursue such transformations further.

Clear enough also are the transformations and rewritings required by the *setting* adopted for any narrative. Σ_2 was set in an upper-middle-class school in a particular city in a very distinctive country in the 1920s and 1930s. These facts must control a great deal of the full contents. They require the insertion of characteristic descriptions and incidents, they control the detailed amplification of the characters, and they continuously modify the dialogue. This they do by reference always (though not exclusively) to the patterns of what should perhaps be called by the barbarous word *causalization* (the allotting of causes and effects, throughout the work, such as have already been discussed). If an incident of speech is not 'in keeping' with where the narrative is set, there will seem to be no way in which it can have been caused. It cannot belong to the partially ordered set of the novel; *pro tanto* it will destroy the structure of the novel. In this respect, the proliferation of the text will be a two-way process: causalization calls for setting, and once a particular setting is decided upon it will require and create elaborate constraints in respect of all the causal structures (even if some of these relate to human nature in general rather than human behaviour in the place and time of the setting).

The processes of 'causalization' are in fact more sustained and intricate still: because the crucial events in a narrative arise out of, and are integrated into the whole narrative by, a mass of detail which prepares for them and which converges upon them from every part of the book. This need for *immersion* of the crucial incidents in an ocean of causality (not for verisimilitude, necessarily: perhaps for more structuring, simply) is what calls for proliferation of the incidents, even the most incidental of them. Beyond this, the process of causalization extends to the calling forth of details which have no direct causal bearing whatever upon the crucial incidents, but which reinforce our acceptance of the causal forces operative in these crucial incidents by providing us with *analogies* to such forces, which we are shown in quite other areas of experience.

This rather general point may be illustrated more in detail by the passages in chapter 2 of Σ_2, which describes the schoolgirls' first walk through the Old Town of Edinburgh:

> Now they were in a great square, the Grassmarket, with the Castle, which was in any case everywhere, rearing between a big gap in the houses where the aristocracy used to live. It was Sandy's first experience of a foreign country, which intimates itself by its new smells and shapes and its new poor. A man sat on the icy-cold pavement; he just sat. A crowd of children, some without shoes, were playing some fight game, and some boys shouted after Miss Brodie's violet-clad company, with words that the girls had not heard before but rightly understood to be obscene. Children and women with shawls came in and out of the dark closes. Sandy found she was holding Mary's hand in her bewilderment, all the girls were holding hands, while Miss Brodie talked of history. Into the High Street, and 'John Knox,' said Miss Brodie, 'was an embittered man. He could never be at ease with the gay French Queen. We of Edinburgh owe a lot to the French. We are Europeans.' The smell was amazingly terrible. In the middle of the road farther up the High Street a crowd was gathered. 'Walk past quietly,' said Miss Brodie.[8]

How can such a passage be seen as the product of generative or transformatory instructions or rules, given by the author to herself, and operating continuously throughout the work?

First of all, some such passage is required somewhere in the work by the crucial incident in chapter 6, where Sandy is finally alienated from her mentor: 'Sandy was bored, it did not seem

8. Penguin ed. (London, 1973), pp. 32–3.

necessary that the world should be saved, only that the poor people in the streets and slums of Edinburgh should be relieved.' The incident presented in the passage quoted above is part, even in its smallest details, of the causalizing preparation for this moment. That is to say, it lies among the causal antecedents of Sandy's moment of rejection: both as to what she thinks is necessary, and as to what she thinks is not. Beyond this, other details in the passage either prepare, or confirm, other points in the narration as a whole. The girls instinctively hold hands: at this moment of time they are 'little' girls. That they know, however, that the language they hear is obscene both sustains, and prepares for, the reader's growing awareness of their growing up. Upon this fact the dénouement rigorously depends. The several contributions made by Miss Brodie's *oratio recta* in the passage quoted need not be laboured. The reference above to *analogies* of the causal forces operative directly in the tale is illustrated by how the slum children are playing 'some fight game'. The causality of the main narrative sequence is made more integral to that sequence, as the reader is reminded that all children are aggressive, and so is prepared to accept (i.e., recognize the causal validity of) the crucial moments of aggressiveness among Miss Brodie's children.

Thus the structure of the narrative optionally (in the sense indicated above, p. 94) determines the detail, and so the structure, of the final full text: we move *from narrative structure across to text structure*. Seemingly trivial phrases like 'some without shoes' (setting), 'we are Europeans' (causalization, since this is all one with Miss Brodie's meaningless pseudocult of Hitler, Leonardo, *et al.*), and tone (because for the author to catch, ironically, these reverberations in her character's 'idiolect' is part of what confirms our sense of her relation to her characters, her story, and indeed ourselves her readers) are *called forth* by standing principles, that is to say, continuously applicable operational rules, in accordance with which the text may be seen as created. As the writer, successively (in the purely conceptual model of composition here envisaged) rewriting, gropes and moves toward, and closes in upon, the final version of the text, such phrases become necessary additions at one point or another. Once in, their deletion would be contrary to the principles upon which the work is being progressively constructed: further transformations cannot readily remove them.

The problems now under examination may be further clarified

by considering the passage in chapter 4 of Σ_2 (that which describes the girls' early months in the Senior School) first *without*, and then *with*, the following sentence:

> By the summer term, to starve off the onslaughts of boredom, and to reconcile the necessities of the working day with their love for Miss Brodie, Sandy and Jenny had begun to apply their new-found knowledge to Miss Brodie in a merry fashion. 'If Miss Brodie was weighed in air and then in water . . .'[9]

This turn of thought is no idle witticism. By the rules governing this composition, an *idle* witticism would require to be rewritten into something like those very words: 'Sandy . . . had begun to *apply* . . . new-found knowledge to Miss Brodie'. The process is a continuing one. By chapter 6 it is occurring at a crucial point in the narrative, in respect of quite other 'new-found knowledge', and in 'merry fashion' no longer, but with the insight, distaste, and youthful self-assurance which are prelude to 'betrayal':

> She thinks she is Providence, thought Sandy, she thinks she is the God of Calvin, she sees the beginning and the end. And Sandy thought, too, the woman is an unconscious Lesbian. . .

In a word: one is accustomed to notice, in any close reading of a passage taken in isolation in a narrative text, how the details lead on to, or out from, other parts of that text, especially the crucial parts of it. Conversely, every crucial part of a text calls, in self-justification, for the pervasive structuring of local texture throughout. Insofar as local details of the text have as their interest that they are creating, sustaining, or densening the whole causal edifice of the novel and, hence, inevitably its verisimilitude, we may say that, over a very wide arc of fiction as we have it, verisimilitude *is* structure.

In the matter of the vertical transformations into which (it is suggested) one may analyse the progression in principle from the summary to the full final text, almost nothing has been said here of one important transformation. I have spoken of causalization, and similarly one could speak of the 'moralization' of the summary narrative sequence (the two are distinguishable in principle). Needless to say, 'moralization' would be an operation to be distinguished in principle and for the purposes of analysis: in practice no author, surely, would settle down to 'moralize his

9. *Ibid.* p. 84.

song' as a separate stage in the process of actual composition. Σ_2 would not be a good novel to choose in this particular context. One may call it a book that leaves its value structure relatively open and free, or (less sympathetically) one that has little to say in such matters. One could not, I think, say the same of Σ_1. Isherwood's novel is far indeed from labouring its moral discriminations, but it is undeniable that there is much to admire in Oliver's character, and much more (I find) to condemn in Patrick's. On the other hand, there is surely no difficulty in envisaging a successful novel which portrays a character who is a publisher and film-maker, and who (though married) has a youthful homosexual lover, as a man to admire – some may reject this, but not I should think on reflection – and an Englishman who goes to India and becomes a Hindu monk as despicable. In other words, we can see that the basic sequence of events in the narration may leave the moral evaluations which the reader is invited to make of the characters almost wholly undetermined. If this is so, then the idea of transformations which determine the basic sequence of events in one direction morally, or in another, seems particularly appropriate. It must be added that in few works which deserve serious consideration are the moral discriminations which the reader is invited to make by the work as a whole coincident with those he may make as he reads along. The usual situation is a more complex one, in which it seems that there is a set of characters, along with their elaborately causal actions and interactions, and on the other hand something like a set of incipient or emergent conceptions: though these are not conceptions in any simple sense save in the emptiest of fictional moralizings. The ways in which, and degree to which, the relations between these two sets might be envisaged in a structurally systematic way require to be taken up in further discussion.

6

Conclusion: structure and the critic's art

This chapter makes some suggestions about the relations between narrative structure and literary criticism. 'Some suggestions' are vague and modest words, and that is as it should be: the discussions about structure in this book make no claim to be comprehensive, and the same is true of what is said here about structure and criticism. For all that, there is a certain question to which a full answer would be both difficult and important; and to try to say even something limited about it is more than worth while.

Criticism may be understood in many different ways; but of the many distinctions which might be drawn there is really only one that lies at the heart of the discussion. Two distinct kinds of critical activity may be identified, and linked with the names of I. A. Richards on the one hand, and Lawrence on the other. Richards' concern in *Principles of Literary Criticism* was to identify the kind of critical process which itself identifies (and in its turn, evokes) 'The most valuable states of mind'. In such a way of expressing the matter, however, everything depends on how the value of a state of mind is understood. For Richards, the most valuable states of mind are those 'which involve the widest and most comprehensive co-ordination of activities' (p. 59).[1] Those words have become well known, and so have Richards' accounts of the elaborately complex co-ordinations which may locate themselves in the literary work, and which in his view enter into the successful reading process.

If criticism is understood along the lines of Richards' discussion, then it seems that a problem barely arises about whether or not literary structures, or more particularly narrative structures, interest the critic. True enough, the kinds of structures which

1. Compare also the references to 'organization' (pp. 50, 57), 'coordination' (pp. 50, 52), and 'systematization' (pp. 50, 51, 56, 57).

have chiefly been discussed here are not the kind that pre-occupied Richards: but any structure which may be recognized in a complex object is *prima facie* something that organizes, and introduces 'co-ordination' among, the parts of that object. From this point of view criticism would be a varied and more or less open-ended activity; as indeed it is in practice. Perhaps some 'projections' of co-ordination would be more interesting to critics than others. Some critics might think that the structures and co-ordinations which psychoanalytic modes of thinking threw up were central, others might think them at best peripheral. There could be many variations of view. The general idea, though, that to a greater or lesser degree what may be seen as a structure would be relevant and interesting for this kind of criticism is plain enough.

There is something which needs to be contrasted with all this. Perhaps it is misleading to think of it as another *kind* of criticism: rather, it is another part of the whole range of activity that the critic can undertake. But it is something of quite special import-ance, something which I believe must be seen in the end as the nerve and life of the critic's task.

One way of identifying what this is would be to raise a question that is not often raised about the three *moments* of the major creative novelist's consciousness, as these are intimated by Leavis in the introductory chapter of *The Great Tradition*. The reference in Leavis's book is of course to the consciousness of the creative writer, not the critic; but the one is a natural clue to the other. The three things that Leavis mentions are a 'vital capacity for experi-ence', a 'reverent openness before life', and 'marked moral inten-sity';[2] and the question is whether these three qualities of con-sciousness necessarily and naturally go together. Why should this be taken for granted? At the very least, the key terms in the three descriptions ('vital', 'reverent' 'intensity' and the like) may need to be understood in certain specific ways, if tension between them is not to arise.

Surely this is in fact the case, moreover. Everyone is familiar with kinds of moral intensity which destroy reverent openness or anything like it. For the three qualities, or criteria, or however it is best to describe them, to come together without tension, 'moral intensity' must be understood (as it perfectly well may be under-

2. *The Great Tradition* (1948), p. 9.

stood) in one distinctive way rather than another. Its meaning must be developed in a certain direction: a direction, it might well turn out, divergent from the sort of moral understanding that goes with expressions like, say, 'moral system'.

The sense that there are two almost contrasting modes of working of the moral consciousness is one that some creative writers have often expressed; some critics have made it into the nerve of their work. Lawrence often responds like this, both as creative writer and as critic. In his essay entitled *The Flying Fish*, for example, he distinguishes the 'ordinary sun', and the ordinary day, of our normal consciousness, from the 'Greater Day' and the 'inward sun' of what is in fact a *'vital* capacity for experience'; and he speaks of 'the despair that comes when the lesser day hems in the greater'. The flying fish is Lawrence's symbol for this vital mode of awareness. It survives in the thinner environment of the air, because always revived from the richer, denser element of the water – 'the great peace of the deeper day'.

In his *Study of Thomas Hardy*, Lawrence responds to this idea as a critic. Throughout that essay he is seeking to identify and stress the two levels at which he sees Hardy's own mind at work: that of the conventional and co-ordinated, of 'proven, deposited experience', and that on the other hand of the 'palpitating leading-shoot of life'. 'The eternal powerful fecundity worked on heedless of him and his arrogance', he writes of Clym Yeobright. It is also in the *Study of Thomas Hardy* that Lawrence – it is one of his most striking critical remarks – makes the same distinction over Aeschylus's *Eumenides:* 'although in his consciousness Aeschylus makes the Furies hideous and Apollo supreme, yet in his own self he makes the Furies wonderful and noble . . . and Apollo a trivial sixth-form braggart'. Doubtless Lawrence is struggling here to express a distinction for which the words will not easily come. 'Consciousness' and 'self' may not be the ideal contrast. But his remark is to the point, because the supremacy of Apollo and of his morality is the order that Aeschylus at least ostensibly imposes on his material, the 'co-ordination' that he appears to be creating within it; whereas for the Furies to be 'wonderful and noble' and Apollo contemptible seems to be a movement away from organization and towards nothing short of chaos.

Critics have repeatedly made their work depend on this sort of contrast: distinguishing the order and co-ordination they find in their author, from a real nerve of first-handedness and life: and coming down in the end (as how could one not when the terms are either so loaded, or – is it? – so revealing) on the side of the latter. In *English Literature in Our Time and the University* Leavis wrote that the student 'needs a principle of life to guide, animate and organize his growing knowledge. . . I think of "principle of life" as something that can't be stated at all'.[3]

There is a celebrated phrase in T. S. Eliot's essay on Jonson. It has been on everyone's lips, though fewer remember what follows it. Eliot says that in the organization of Jonson's verse something is lacking. What is lacking is the intricately co-ordinated complexity Eliot found in certain of Jonson's contemporaries. He refers to this co-ordinated complexity in words that Richards must have found congenial, and that have been cited, times without number, by those who have expounded the sort of critical enterprise Richards invited us to endorse. '*A network of tentacular roots. . . .*' Eliot however did not leave the matter there. The words he used to complete his sentence are much less in a Richards vein (there is no need to claim that Richards would repudiate them, that is quite another matter); and they raise possibilities of tension in the meaning of the whole sentence much like those which were suggested, earlier on, over 'reverent openness' as against 'moral intensity'. 'A network of tentacular roots *reaching down to the deepest terrors and desires*'.[4]

Is it not precisely here that a major problem presents itself? 'Roots' may be a metaphor that leads on easily enough to the closing words of the phrase: but Richards' 'co-ordination' lies quite as much, if not more, in the other metaphor, the 'network'. Does the network of *co-ordinations* really reach down to those deepest terrors and desires which are one with our vital capacity for experience, with the greater day and the inward sun, the eternal powerful fecundity? If (as seems likely enough) network and co-ordination belong rather with 'proven, deposited experience' and all that goes with that, when the discussion returns to the theme of this book the answer it reaches may be a dispiriting one; and analyses of narrative structure, while they may well enter such networks with ease, will direct away from, rather than towards, what was called just now the 'nerve and life' of the critic's task.

It would be wrong to think that what has been taken over the

3. *op. cit.* (1969), p. 136.
4. 'Ben Jonson': in *Selected Essays, 1917–1932* (1932), p. 155.

last few pages as the nerve and life of the critic's work is no more than a twentieth-century or Lawrence–Leavis preoccupation. If we allow for differences of vocabulary we can recognize it in one critic after another. It is in Matthew Arnold when he praises 'the *extraordinary power* with which Wordsworth feels the *joy* offered to us . . . in the simple *primary* affections and duties', or writes of how we can cure ourselves of false valuations over literature by letting our minds 'rest upon that great and *inexhaustible word life*', until we enter into its meaning. It seems to underlie Arnold's claim in 'The Study of Poetry' that 'the best poetry will be found to have a power of forming, sustaining, and delighting us *as nothing else can*'. On reflection, there proves even to be a quite significant analogy between, on the one hand, 'delighting' in such a way as also to be 'sustaining' and 'forming', and the deepest 'terrors' and 'desires' on the other.

The same ultimate conception of the true literary work is visible also when Wordsworth writes that the purpose of his ballads is to trace 'the *primary* laws of our nature' and to reveal 'the *essential passions of the heart*'; or that poems of enduring value come from long and deep thought in a mind of 'more than usual organic sensibility'; or that a poet is one who, more than other men, 'rejoices . . . in the *spirit of life* that is in him'; or when he sees the pleasure-giving aspect of poetry as nothing short of 'an acknowledgement of the beauty of the *universe*'. All these various phrases have deeper reverberations that lead outwards and downwards to something like Eliot's 'deepest terrors and desires'.

In this context, Hopkins is of quite special interest. When he writes: 'There lives the *dearest freshness* deep down things' ('God's Grandeur'), or says that he '. . . caught [the windhover] in his riding . . . *in his ecstasy*', he also is expressing an intuition of primary affirmation of energy: this time not in the literary work, but in external realities that entered into his own verse. That being so, there is a good deal of interest in what Hopkins saw as the fundamental immediate (as against ultimate) source of such an emanation of energy: it bears in a significant way on the present question.

For Hopkins, the concept of 'inscape' was something that could show in a natural object or in a work of art, and sometimes the latter could illuminate the former:

> at a little timber bridge I looked at some delicate flying shafted

ashes – there was one especially of single *sonnet-like inscape* (*Journal*, ed. C. C. Abbott, 10 September 1874)

Probably there is no need to prove in detail how inscape for Hopkins was one with the beauty of the object and the release of its unique energy to the spectator:

> I do not think I have ever seen anything more *beautiful* than the bluebell I have been looking at. I know the beauty of our Lord by it. Its inscape is *mixed of strength and grace* (18 May 1870)

For Hopkins, inscape here was the route to an absolutely primal creativity, and once again, 'strength' and 'grace' have mingled overtones like those noticed already. Other examples are:

> Dielytras – in the full-blow flower there are at least four symmetrical 'wards' all *beautiful* in inscape (14 June 1872)

> I saw the inscape through *freshly*, as if my eye were still growing, though with a companion the eye and the ear are for the most part shut and *instress cannot come* (12 December 1872)

> standing before the gateway I had *an instress which only the true old work gives* from the *strong* and noble inscape of the pointed arch. (11 November 1874)

Every reader of Hopkins will know how much more there is in his writings that draws the ideas of inscape, beauty and felt vitality (one aspect of 'instress') into association. But beyond this, Hopkins continually associates inscape, and the power and beauty of inscape, with organization and order. What, in other words, is creating it for him is what it is reasonable to call *structure*:

> This skeleton inscape of a spray-end of ash . . . is worth noticing *for the suggested globe*. (25 August 1870)

This remark is elucidated by a sketch. The point in Hopkins' mind is that the half-realized, underlying shape of the spray is a spherical one. Or again:

> in . . . the broken blobs of snow . . . I could find a square scaping in which helped the eye over another *hitherto disordered field of things*. (14 March 1871)

or:

> I looked at the groin or the flank [of a horse] and saw how the set of the hair *symmetrically flowed outwards from it* to all parts of the body, so that, following that one may inscape the whole beast very simply. (6 April 1874)

What Hopkins has observed is the order of structure of the horse's hide as a whole; and the idea of 'symmetry' (doubtless the two flanks of the horse) comes immediately to him in connection with it. Occasionally Hopkins puts the point explicitly and in abstract terms:

> Now it is the virtue of *design, pattern or inscape* to be distinctive (Letter to Bridges, 15 February 1879)

If the various ideas brought forward so far are drawn together, three guiding conceptions emerge. The first is of what I have called the 'nerve and life' of the critic's task: to identify and remain alive to a certain fundamental quality, or mode of consciousness, in the work. The second is that a sense of this mode and of its importance may be identified, more or less explicitly, in the writings of many distinguished critics. The third is the possibility, emerging clearly enough from Hopkins' dependence on the idea of inscape, that structure, so far from being alien to that mode of consciousness, may in one way or another be closely involved with it. This suggestion will not commend itself to all. One sometimes encounters, among those concerned with literature, a quite general rejection of the very idea of 'structure' or 'structuralism'. One example of this is an article by George Watson entitled *Chomsky: What has it to do with literature?* (*TLS*; 14 February 1975). It is not easy to identify the exact target of Mr Watson's dislike here; and in part, perhaps, this results from a defect in the article by Chomsky himself, on which Watson's discussion is entirely based. Chomsky, in the opening page of an article in *College English*, 1966 ('The Current Scene in Linguistics'),[5] identified 'structural linguistics' with 'descriptive linguistics' of a kind that rejects any *pre*-scriptive dimension. That was already a controversial definition of structural linguistics. Later, Chomsky concedes that descriptive linguistics is concerned not only with the 'types of elements' in a given language, but also 'the constraints that they obey' which is in effect a prescriptive dimension after all. At this later stage it seems that the essential defect in descriptive linguistics is in Chomsky's view something else: its inability to offer *explanations* of particular constraints, explanations based upon more and more general principles of universal grammar; upon 'human mental structure'; and in the end, upon general physiology. In referring to these broader issues, however, Chomsky

5. Reprinted in *Literary English Since Shakespeare*, ed. G. Watson, 1970.

re-uses the word 'structure' ('the study of particular grammars will be fruitful only in so far as it is based on a precisely articulated theory of *linguistic structure*') in a favourable sense, and one that cannot at all be identified with what is descriptive only.

Thus Chomsky's discussion in this essay (he has of course greatly extended it elsewhere) seems not to be wholly explicit in regard to what is 'structural' or 'structuralist', and what if anything is wrong with being that. But Watson takes Chomsky's essay as amounting simply to a 'demolition of structuralism' – to use his own phrase – which is simply an emancipation at once of the student of literature, and of the student of language. The two can come together and work together because 'structuralism' is demolished. 'Structuralism', in his discussion, seems to mean everything and anything. At one point, what has gone with Chomsky's demolition is French *Nouvelle Critique*, at another it is an unexplained 'literary structuralism', or even 'Modern Critical Thought' in general. Why any of these are dependent upon the exclusive validity of non-prescriptive grammar is left unexplained. What transpires ultimately is just a comprehensive rejection of anything that uses the idea of 'structure', or perhaps only that uses the word. The discussion is simply not worth pursuing at this level.

If one attempts to pursue it at a more significant level, there is perhaps a preliminary point to be made. If 'structure' means not simply 'form' as that term has been used traditionally of works of art in general and of literary works in particular, but something that (though it may well be associated with 'form' traditionally understood) is itself a matter of abstract relations or complexes of relations, it is likely to call for the use of *technical terms*. Some critics believe that this necessarily does harm; but to think so is excessively pessimistic. Introducing such terms can no doubt reveal, or encourage, a frame of mind quite alien to the vital concerns of the literary critic. It may also be true that since criticism itself is hard, and bandying technical terms idly about is easy, to use such terms may harm beginner students. But to think that simply because this is so (if it is indeed so) they are better avoided altogether, is to identify the teaching process, even the earlier stages of it, with the central concerns of the critic: the two are much related, but they are not identical. Further than that, a technical term no more intrinsically (as against fortuitously) induces a mechanical and non-critical or anti-critical attitude in the enquirer, than does any other term.

The objection may be put in another form. It may be argued that such expressions as 'supposition' and its co-relative 'pro-pone', or 'initiative' and 'response', employed in earlier chapters, tend to conceal and ignore the differences and nuances of tone, of stress and insistence, of feeling and 'keeping' (or planned lack of it) which are so much part of the art of the author and the complex power of the work. Yet, put this way, the argument is not complaining of a harmful tendency connected with the use of a word specially introduced, but of what is integral to the very act of classifying. The process of assimilating the not-identical is part of the process of conceptualization itself. It occurs all the time, almost whatever words are used, and equally whether they are technical terms or what seem to us as non-technical as you can get: the primary and indispensable vocabulary of talking about fiction ('character', 'scene', 'setting', say) or indeed, literature in general ('rhythm', 'realize', 'tone', 'style'). Locke distinguishes between wit, that discovers likenesses among un-likes, and judgement that discriminates differences among what is like.[6] To engage in either of these mental activities is not to reject the other. To promulgate a law that literary illumination is always promoted by being sensitive to shades and nuances, and never by assimilating respects of sameness which they overlie and conceal, would be the most peremptory and sweeping of all possible acts of standardiz-ing assimilation.

But, especially in an Anglo-Saxon context, specifically narra-tive structures may well be seen by many as at a kind of standing disadvantage or rather discount. There is likely to be an idea that they necessarily mean less than features or structures of another kind; that this other kind will be what brings us nearest to the nerve and life of a literary work; and that specifically narrative features and structures will inevitably divert the reader's response away from the central regenerative energies of the work and towards what is formalistic or even factitious in regard to it.

This way of thinking is likely to be based on what is often put forward as *the* central, guiding conception with regard to the literary work: that it is made out of language. Here therefore will lie its central and decisive organizations. If it has 'reverent open-

6. *Essay Concerning Human Understanding*, II. xi. 2.

ness' or 'vital capacity', if it shows a palpitating 'leading-shoot of
life', if it reaches to the 'deepest terrors and desires' or both
delights and forms as nothing else can, that will come from how it
draws upon the marvellous and profound powers of human
language. We shall turn our backs on its central and life-giving
forces if we look anywhere else.

There is no need to deny that, simply from the fact that it uses
words and so has contact with the great and mysterious powers
that lie in the using of words, any work of literature may have
access to unique powers of forming and delighting, to what reaches
down to the deepest terrors and desires. But to say so is not the
same as to say that this is the only or even the most powerful way in
which such a work may gain access to those powers and sources
of life. The point may be made clear through a distinction which
Aristotle makes, with characteristic terseness, at the beginning of
the *Poetics* (i.3):

> Epic poetry, and tragic-drama poetry, and also comedy and
> choral odes and the major part of flute-music and harp-music,
> may all be seen generally as imitation; but they differ from each
> other in three respects: either they imitate different things; or,
> they imitate *with* different things; or, they imitate in different
> ways, not the same way

When it is said that the decisive fact about works of literature is
that they are *written in words*, what is being called to mind is the
second of the set of three points that Aristotle makes in that
passage (the point comes first in order in the Greek text) and the
reference is what is sometimes termed the *medium* of expression in
which the work is composed. But the *mode* of expression is a
conception which invites one to recall the fact (it was surely in
Aristotle's mind as he wrote that sentence) that works in many
different media – 'they imitate in different ways' – may all be in
the narrative mode. There may be narrative works, for example,
in the media of words, or of directly imitative gestures (mime), or
of continuous photography (silent film), or of more or less styl-
ized dance-movements (ballet). Any such work, regardless of the
medium in which it is created, belongs to the class of works in the
narrative mode and may have such powers as membership of that
class gives it. It will belong to one class of works by virtue of its
medium, and have access to such powers as this membership may
give it; but that does not call in question either its membership of

the class of works in the narrative mode, and access to such powers as are open to it from that; or, that the powers of the narrative mode, and of such narrative organizations and structures as distinguish that mode, may be not trivial but massive.

There is no doubt that the powers available to a work, because its medium is language, may be massive. Language, for men, seems almost as if it were coeval and co-authoritative with consciousness. We know, true enough, that words can be used so that they lack their seemingly natural creative powers and depths; even, that their powers for creativity are supplanted by powers only for destruction (and initially, in this case, for self-destruction). But when this happens it does not seem an accident; rather, it is as if perverse social or personal forces have dwindled or destroyed what would otherwise be great. This is a large subject, it has been under discussion since Plato's *Cratylus*, and it need not be pursued here because it is the other side of the matter which is at issue: is there any reason to suppose that creative and life-affirming powers comparable with those made available to art through the *medium* of words, may also and distinguishably be made available to art through the *mode* of narrative, and – more particularly – through the structures and organizations that may be recognized within that mode?

Certain points support this possibility. The first is a preliminary one which is important in itself though it requires to be made briefly because it is not exactly germane. The narrative mode has access to the most powerful forces and drives in life because of the 'what' that it imitates, the 'things' that make up its subject-matter. Narratives may of course imitate the trivial; but certainly the most important realities in human affairs, of what engage men's deepest terrors and desires, and also their most potent – and indeed most affirmative – emotions, call for embodiment in the narrative mode. Perhaps they most particularly do so: more so than anything else, or than they themselves call for any other mode of presentation.

In respect of content, then, narrative ought very much to bring into literature that 'vital capacity', that Lawrentian being 'alight with life', which criticism can ignore only with disaster to itself.

That, however, relates to narrative content; not to narrative structure. About narrative structure, it has to be said that much has been written on this subject by those who seem unaware of the deepest, most fructifying concerns of criticism, and seem sometimes to show a spirit aridly hostile to those concerns. But the same has been true also of a vast body of criticism that has started off from the idea that it is being made out of *words*, and drawing on the powers of words, that is the whole and sole key to literary creativity. Whatever is done, one must remember, doing it well and so as fully to be true to itself is rare; while the opposite is common.

There remain certain considerations which suggest that structures may be found in narrative which indeed come close to the critic's deepest and most creative concerns.

There is a general connection between the degree to which structure in the literary work can connect with the deepest terrors and desires or embody and so evoke the mind's reverent openness before life, and the degree to which experience and consciousness are seen in something like Kantian terms. To think of 'Kantian terms' in this context means simply the fundamental idea that the forms and structures of experience are not imposed wholesale on the mind from the reality which lies outside it, but at least in part represent the mind's own permanent nature and what in consequence are the standing possibilities of our consciousness. If those aspects of our experience have the form, or the structure, that they do have, because those forms and structures represent something deep and permanent within ourselves that enters into our experiences and moulds those experiences into the general patterns that it has of itself, then it is simple enough to see how those forms and structures can embody and therefore evoke the most alive and creative part of the mind, the 'Greater day and the inward sun' of the psyche.

In fact, it would almost be paradoxical to think that what is so deeply and permanently and centrally embedded in the self as to be constructive and constitutive of its experience in general should be an automatic, routine, un-living part of the self; and that the 'leading-shoot of life' (to use Lawrence's expression again) should be something relatively more passive, more receptive, more dependent upon external variation.

Furthermore, if that train of thought holds for our experience in general, it must hold equally for our experience of art and in particular for our experience of works of literature: and it is difficult not to agree that we have a sense of this, as part in fact of the experience of reading. The *content* or the *detail* of literary works may often seem to be what lies behind our being absorbed and engrossed in the literary work (Johnson's 'restless and unquenchable curiosity') or what brings us transient moments of, say, intense poignancy or delighted surprise; but the experiences which seem to be the most massive and profound parts of our reading experience are other than these 'whodunit' excitements. They involve some total re-projection of the work: or some definitive falling-into-place of its overall perspective, which on analysis is likely to prove to be the *epiphenomenon* of structure, or structure the epiphenomenon, maybe, of it.

In reflecting on this point, moreover, one must notice that in a certain general way our experience of works of art ought inherently and intrinsically to be more comprehensively *more* 'Kantian' in quality than our experience in general: for the structures that we find in the work (one recalls Wordsworth's phrase, in another context, 'both what we find, and what we half create') have originally been implanted there by a mind which was much like our own in its 'deepest terrors and desires', its whole 'spirit of life', quite as much as in its fundamental modes, philosophically speaking, of perception or conceptualization. A large question might be raised about the systematic relation between the general apprehension of reality by the individual consciousness, and its particular apprehension of the work of art, which is a creation of one individual consciousness re-animated, as it were, in apprehension by another individual consciousness which in fundamental ways is the twin of the first. But I shall not pursue this abstruse matter.

Perhaps something can be said at this stage about the relation between structures of *language* in a literary work, and narrative structures. The point is important in itself, and also a helpful introduction to what needs to be said about narrative structures. Let us assume that we are reasonably clear as to what we mean by organization, or structure, or 'pattern' in a work. We may have in mind a constellation of key terms which occur pervasively through the work: not at random but in some articulated scheme of semantic relations which itself brings in a structure. We may mean patterns of imagery, and speak of 'patterns', not just occurrences, because again we see relations of equivalence, gradation, polarization and so on between these, and so once again are concerned with matters of relation and so of structure. We may have irony in mind, and if we call this a matter of language because irony is generated from what might be termed semantic micro-tensions, it is also true that the 'extension' of ironic state-ments, and their inter-relations, are matters of structure. Or we may be thinking of the organizing of different styles in a work – perhaps, even, nothing more than the alternation of prose and verse in it, or some other equally basic language-feature.

Whatever feature of the language of the work is in question, however, if the work is a narrative work a certain important fact seems to follow. In this case, there must in some sense or other (unless the narrative is a meaningless chaos) be a narrative struc-ture; and then, in proportion as anything which presents itself as specifically a structure of *language* becomes prominent and important in the work, the likelihood that it will enter into relation with that narrative structure increases, until with any truly prominent and important linguistic structure, that likeli-hood becomes certainty. Putting this in more general terms: so far from 'language' being the key to literary interpretation, and nar-rative structure an abstract irrelevance to the critic's central con-cerns – given a narrative, language tends, of the nature of the case, to become one of the narrative facts.

What is the reason for this? On the face of it, it seems likely enough, and one might suppose that it stood as an inductive generalization from empirical observation of a number of indi-vidual literary works. But I think it will be seen on reflection to be a necessary and *a priori* truth: and – therefore (since I do not wish to claim it as a 'synthetic' *a priori* truth), if it is often overlooked, that is because we have allowed a complex critical terminology and credulously established presuppositions to blind us to the true inter-relations of our own critical vocabulary.

The reason for suggesting that between what is linguistic and what is narrative there is this logically necessary connection may be approached as follows. Suppose there is a linguistic feature which it was impossible to see as in any way related to the narrative structure of the work: in respect of what has been asserted, that is to say, a negative, a counter-example. Now suppose that the author revises his work, over and over, in a series of new versions such that in each member of the series of re-visions, the given linguistic feature becomes always more and more prominent. Now suppose, finally, that the absence of rela-tion to the narrative structure of the work is somehow maintained. Is this last supposition not a self-contradiction? Surely the very absence of relation that the narrative has to this ever more and more prominent feature of the language in which the narrative is narrated, must itself become a significant part of the narrative. A narrative organization which as it were remains always rebutted, always repudiated, always set at nought, by an organization in the work which both runs parallel to it, and is all-pervasive and all-prominent, is a narrative organization which exists under something like a permanent disclaimer. It simply cannot be the same narrative organization as otherwise it would be. There must be a degree to which that other and non-communicating organization ironically modulates it to a joke, or a self-conscious convention, or a vehicle for something other than itself, or whatever else it may be of the kind. And quite simply: that ironical modulating *is a relation*.

The only possible alternative to that, is for the unity of the whole work to cease to exist. If this does not happen, then the fact that in a narrative there is some great central reality which allegedly has no bearing on that narrative, itself says something about that narrative after all. The very fact of having-no-bearing must have a bearing of a higher order; and what has a bearing on something is in a relation to it; and so such a language feature *necessarily becomes part of the narrative structure*.

One example may elucidate this. In Swift's *Tale of a Tub* the non-narrative sections are far more extensive, and also far more remarkable in other ways, than the narrative proper. As a result, one's impression on first reading may be bewilderment. The work seems not be a single and unified work at all, but mainly a series of 'Digressions'. Fuller acquaintance restores the unity of the work, but does so by finding ways in which the 'Digressions' (not all, of course, actually labelled such) profoundly modify the meaning of the narrative. They become, that is to say, part of the narrative structure. *A Tale of a Tub* is an extreme case which perhaps makes clear how the very unrelatedness of language-organizations to narrative-organization must either terminate the unity of the work, or in the end become a relevance, a relatedness, of its own.

One may go further, in fact, and argue that Swift's title for this work was itself an invitation to the reader to reflect on these very possibilities and to identify how they work themselves out. In 1575 George Gascoyne, in effect thinking about both narrative structure and structures in language (his own terminology is of course quite different from that) wrote:

> What Theame so ever you do take in hande; if you do handle it
> but *tanquam in oratione perpetua*, and never study for some depth
> of device in ye Invention, & some figures also in the handlying
> thereof: it will appeare to the skilfull Reader but *a tale of a tubbe*.[7]

'A tale of a tub' was a proverbial expression for a narrative that
had no order, structure or resolution: but first Jonson, in his late
play 'A Tale of a Tub', invited the reader or spectator to find some
kind of sense and meaning, anyhow, in what was ostensibly no
more than that; and then Swift used the same title for a work
which, far more deeply and ambitiously, challenged the reader to
find order where at first there seemed to be none.

Thus the first of the two reasons why narrative structure can
work powerfully towards the critic's deepest concerns, the 'nerve
and life' of his enterprise, is that as any other, non-narrative
feature of a work waxes larger and larger, either the narrative
structure must find a place for that feature and enter into relation
with it: or, the structure as a whole must break down and the
work cease to be a single narrative. But therefore if a work is a
narrative work, there must in some way or another be a narrative
structure that embraces and *integrates the whole of it*. A work may
show structural patterns in this or that part of itself, but that
cannot be all there is to say. In the end, either it is not a single
narrative at all; or, along some projection, there must be one
single structure embracing the whole. Smaller structural patterns
are parts of larger ones, and the largest narrative structures must
therefore be as large as the whole work, and be completed and
resolved insofar as it is itself resolved.

Thus if anything at all both reflects, and perhaps indeed creates,
the largest-scale, most decisive, and so most powerful design of a
work, it is the narrative structure which does so. What then more
than this very thing is likely to manifest 'the Greater Day and the
Deeper Sun' of the novel?

That point relates to the size and extent of the narrative structures of a work. Their large, indeed all-embracing size and extent
makes it likely that they will embody the author's deepest and
most vital concerns. The complementary point relates not to the
scale of narrative structures, but to their essentially dynamic
nature: their concern intrinsically with change, transformation,
revelation, resolution. This other consideration, which argues

7. *Certayne Notes of Instruction concerning the making of verse or ryme in
English. Works*, ed. J. W. Cunliffe, 1907–10, vol. II, p. 465.

more strongly still that matters of narrative structure, so far from pointing away from the critic's deepest concern over the literary work, are likely to converge massively upon it, may be approached through another of the remarks that Hopkins makes, in his *Journal*, about *inscape*:

> A beautiful instance of inscape sided on the slide, that is successive sidings of one inscape, is seen in the behaviour of the flag flower from the shut bud to the full blowing: each term you can distinguish is beautiful in itself and of course if the whole 'behaviour' were gathered up and so stalled it would have a beauty of all the higher degree. (13 June 1871)

A 'siding' is for Hopkins a modification or variation of some basic reality, whether it is matter of Being in general, particular conformations of rock, or variations in a stanza-pattern.[8] What Hopkins is saying, or in fact taking for granted in this passage, is (in the terminology of the present book) that a related series of structures, if held or stored ('stalled') in the mind as a whole, would give a larger structure of which the emotional power would be 'of all the higher degree'.

Hopkins is thinking in that passage of the opening of a flower into bloom. The structures of a narrative must in the final analysis be of the same kind, and so also have 'a beauty of all the higher degree'. What this means more particularly is that narrative structure, being essentially about changes and resolutions, must essentially be also about what releases, and manifests, and finally orders, some of the greater or perhaps the greatest energies of the work. If one casts one's mind back over some of the earlier essays in the present book, certain exemplifications of this may come to mind. Not all, of course, of the works that have been discussed are likely to bear upon what has been called the nerve and life of the critic's preoccupation. But as what at first presents itself as the racy medley of the latter part of *Crime and Punishment* is seen to be moving with exhaustive definitiveness towards its purgatorial climax, as the gradations and polarizations of *Love Among the Haystacks* or *The Lesson of the Master* progressively assert themselves, as the immense power driving *Phèdre* throughout its concealed enumerations emerges, or *Middlemarch* drives forward its massive processes of proponing and eliminating until its narrative comes to rest as it does – as these things happen, the reader finds

8. *Journals and Papers, ed. cit.*, pp. 130, 155, 267.

himself encountering long and orchestrated movements of great and life-enhancing energies. The greater sun and the deepest terrors and desires, the power and the joy, the spirit of life, generate and manifest themselves in these major narrative integrations in all their reverent capacity and vital openness.

Doubtless the critic's primary act of recognition and salutation for these modes and potentialities of consciousness, in their glowing detail and immediacy, is a more central critical achievement than meticulously to trace out, in abstract or symbolizing terms, the patterns and structures which accompany, resume and diagrammatize those powers and energies. But that is something that the analytical critic, if his work has its measure of interest and worth, will view with equanimity.

APPENDIX 1

Poetic analysis and the idea of the transformation-rule: some examples from Herbert, Wordsworth, Pope and Shakespeare

Much has by now been published by way of attempts to apply linguistic theory to literary criticism. Few are familiar with the whole of it, and I myself am far from that. Explanations are always ready to hand as to why one's knowledge is limited, but in this particular case, it is fair to mention that the critic who turns his attention to this area is likely soon to feel disappointment. He encounters prolix but empty programme-writing, and a good deal also of what in the end yields trivial results or none. Above all, he will have a sense, from the work of many linguists though not all, that the inner force behind attempts to utilize linguistics in criticism is a spirit quite alien to literature. This is a spirit which drives the professional linguist to carve out a new area of operation for his own specialism; or drives a critic to seek something to say when otherwise he would have nothing.

In these circumstances, it is not surprising that students of literature often show an inclination to dismiss linguistics; brushing it aside as something which need not concern them, and feeling free to soldier on as before. Three distinct attitudes thus emerge. First, that of the acquisitive linguist, whose desire is to apply his subject more than to illuminate literature. Then, the critic who seeks self-resuscitation. Last, the critic who seems to relish security against outside contributions. All three attitudes are undesirable, and all result from making the same false assumption. This is, that if linguistic theory has any kind of relevance to literary criticism, it will be because it can be *applied* to literature and the discussion of works of literature, and that more or less automatically and mechanically. The acquisitive linguist and the self-resuscitating critic hope for such an application. The self-secure critic (if I may so put it) decides he can safely turn his back on the whole affair.

I have said enough by way of preliminaries, and I am sorry if they seem diagrammatic. Their purpose is to make it clear that this present discussion attempts something modest in scope, but not exposed, all the same, to the criticism that it seeks to apply linguistics to literature mechanically. It is not exposed to that objection, because its purpose is, in the very first place, to consider whether there is something the critic may derive from linguistics, specifically by rejecting anything like borrowing in particularized terms. Instead, that is, he may learn something by a general contemplation of the linguistic mode of thinking; and use that something, in the distinctive field of criticism, with a difference that proceeds precisely from his own understanding of that distinctiveness. Anything which results from this approach will doubtless seem less of a specialized, professionalized open-sesame than the linguist himself could wish for. That might be the opposite of a defect. There can be a 'mechanical' application of linguistic analysis to literary analysis, which all the same displays subtlety and intelligence. Let me take an example of this, Sol Saporta's article of 1960, 'The Application of Linguistics to the Study of Poetic Language'.[1] Saporta's approach is in a sense very straightforward. Ordinary language is grammatical language, and linguistics studies the rules generating the grammatical sentences which make up a language. Poetry has more than its share of what Saporta (infelicitously it must be said) calls 'lower-order grammaticalness: like "the trees whisper" or "the night fears the boy"'. It seems that this idea originates from an unpublished essay by Noam Chomsky dated 1956. Then, it is implied, just as the linguist can formulate the rules of, shall we say, standard-order grammaticalness giving the sentence of the standard language, so he should be able to formulate other rules which generate the lower-order grammaticalness of poetry. The critic must resist any temptation to say that the salient point about sentences like 'the trees whisper' is something quite other than the crude idea that they are not fully grammatical. Save perhaps at a profound, metaphysical level, this is likely to lead only to verbal dispute.

Saporta's approach is developed by J. P. Thorne, in pieces like 'Stylistics and Generative Grammar' (1965), 'Poetry, Stylistics and Imaginary Grammars' (1969), and 'Generative Grammar and

1. *Style in Language*, ed. T. A. Sebeok (New York, 1960), 82–93.

Stylistic Analysis' (1970).[2] Thorne takes John Donne's 'Nocturnall Upon S. Lucies Day' and Theodore Roethke's 'Dolour' and points out that they contain expressions of 'lower-level grammaticalness' like 'I am the grave of all things' or 'the inexorable sadness of pencils'. But Thorne notices a regularity about these expressions. They occur steadily, throughout the two poems. We could say, Thorne argues, that it is as if a rule is at work, generating, within the language of the poem, the very expressions which the rules of the standard language decline to generate. In the Donne, we could say, the rule is that the first person singular pronoun selects inanimate noun phrases ('the grave', 'every dead thing', 'their epitaph' and so on), whereas of course in standard English this is just the sort of expression that the first person singular pronoun cannot select. In the Roethke, we could say, the rule is that certain nouns ('pencil', 'paperweight', etc.) constitute a new sub-category of nouns, which can be selected by 'sad' and its synonyms; as again is not the case in the standard language. Whether or not this is 'grammar', I leave aside. One can agree to call it grammar, and the crucial difficulty remains for criticism.

This approach clearly has its interest; but in concerning itself with the sort of deviation which concerns the linguist quite generally, it concerns itself with what is peripheral for poetry. This transpires clearly at one point in Thorne's 1970 discussion: 'ungrammatical sentences tend to occur far more frequently in poetry than in prose'. True, but ungrammatical sentences do not occur far more frequently in poetry than grammatical ones. Quite the contrary, it is grammaticalness, in the fullest sense, which has been the staple of poetry, as we all know; and to base one's approach on the occurrence of ungrammaticalness, as René Wellek pointed out in the discussion which followed Saporta's paper when it was first delivered, is to confine oneself to the peripheral, and concentrate on those few poets (G. M. Hopkins, Dylan Thomas, E. E. Cummings), or few poems indeed, which have relied on eccentricity for success, and been freaks great or small.

Another linguist, W. O. Hendricks, has criticized Thorne's concentration on the language of a poem as if this were some-

2. J. P. Thorne, 'Stylistics and Generative Grammar', *Journal of Linguistics*, 1 (1965), 49–59; 'Poetry, Stylistics and Imaginary Grammar', *ibid.*, 5 (1969), 147–50; 'Generative Grammar and Stylistic Analysis', *New Horizons in Linguistics*, ed. J. Lyons (London 1970), 185–98.

thing, a kind of substance, or material, which could be thought of by itself in abstraction. Hendricks declares rightly that the coherence of the individual text, from beginning to middle to end, is the essential starting-point; and certainly, Thorne's remark about the grammatical anomalies he detects in the 'Nocturnall' – 'It seems likely that these linguistic facts underlie the sense of chaos and breakdown of natural order which many literary critics have associated with the poem' – seems to underpin the greater by the lesser. Hendricks writes: 'There must be some principle whereby the images are "bound together" such that any arbitrary reshuffling of them would destroy the coherence of the whole'.[3] Elsewhere, Hendricks explores the concept of textual coherence over units of more than sentence-length.[4] But his attempt, solid as it is, must be called a failure, perhaps because he tried to solve the problem of textual structure and coherence too much in the linguist's exclusive terms. In other words, just as Thorne tried to understand poems simply by considering what linguistics, taken *au pied de la lettre*, could tell him about local deviation within the sentence, so Hendricks relied on linguistics in the same mechanical way to deal with the larger structures of the literary work.

In this whole field, the most rewarding essay which a linguist has written, and which I have read, is Richard Ohmann's 'Generative Grammars and the Concept of Literary Style.[5] This is not because of the interesting stylistic analyses which Ohmann here achieves; though this aspect of his essay deserves commendation. He takes a passage from Faulkner, removes from it the results of certain linguistic operations (systematically 'de-naturing' certain of the operations Faulkner himself may be supposed intuitively to have performed) and by this means shows that these simple operations contain much of the essential 'flavour' of Faulkner's style. Unscramble a passage from Hemingway along the same lines, he then shows, and nothing results. Unscramble this Hemingway passage along other lines, equally simple but relating to its indirect-speech effects instead of its relative-clause and conjunction structure, and Hemingway can be systematically

3. W. O. Hendricks, 'Three Models for a Description of Poetry', *Journal of Linguistics* 5 (1969), 1–22.

4. W. O. Hendricks, 'On the Notion of Beyond the Sentence', *Linguistics*, 37 (1967), 12–51.

5. R. Ohmann, 'Generative Grammars and the Concept of Literary Style', *Word*, 20 (1964), 423–39.

'de-natured' too. Within limits, the whole piece is from this point of view singularly enlightening. The limits are, that once again attention is being directed only to such operations as may be expressed in the normal categories of linguistic theory. There is no question of re-thinking the whole matter of what makes an 'operation' on a sentence-structure, within the quite distinctive context of a work of imaginative literature. The result once again is that what the linguist offers to enlighten about, whether in Faulkner, Hemingway – or James, whom Ohmann refers to briefly – is stylistic idiosyncrasy; and as such it is not what is central to literature but what is peripheral. Indeed, to choose highly 'mannered' authors like Faulkner or Hemingway is like choosing such authors as Cummings or Dylan Thomas, and open to the same objection.

Ohmann's essay introduces a more general idea, which brings me to the main part of my discussion. This is the idea that what will help and interest the critic of literature, when he turns to linguistic theory, is likely to be not the generative rule, but the transformation-rule. Ohmann's first reason for considering the transformation-rule more promising than the generative, or more strictly phrase-structure rule, was that many transformation-rules are optional. There is no choice about putting -*s* for plural; but you can speak active or passive as you prefer. At a technical level, this optional quality has since been questioned; but from the stylistic point of view it remains a valid distinction. Second, Ohmann noted that transformation-rules related to the structures of whole sentences or indeed to complexes of sentences; and that this came nearer than the generative rule (about -*s* for plural, or the definite article and so on) to the kind of thinking the writer engages in. All this seems perfectly sound.

The central question I wish to raise, is this. Ought the critic, in asking himself what use he can make of linguistic theory, simply to consider such transformation-rules as are served up to him ready for use by the linguists? Is there not an alternative to this – one which gives him less direct help, but by that very fact, greater freedom of action and a greater opportunity to concentrate attention on what as a critic he finds poetically important? What I venture to offer is in a sense not the *application* of linguistics to poetic analysis at all: but the point at issue is precisely whether the very idea of application is not disablingly mechanical. My suggestion is that the critic allow his mind to play freely over two general ideas, which indeed come from linguistics in the context of linguistic transformation-rules, as possible helps to poetic analysis in certain cases. These two general ideas are, first, simply the idea of a rule itself; and then, the idea that the kind of rule he may find is operative will be a rule whereby sentences of one form are transformed systematically into sentences of another. I shall proceed to consider a few poems or passages along these lines. To explore these possibilities is not of course to deny that transformation-rules in the linguist's full sense may also help the critic: but only to not assume that either there is that kind of help from linguistics, or none at all.

One should note that neither of the two ideas I am putting forward is immediately very acceptable to the critic. J. J. Katz and P. M. Postal, in *An Integrated Theory of Linguistic Descriptions* (1964), make clear what the idea of a rule involves. They speak of 'stating the domains of transformations in terms of sets of conditions or phrase-markers'.[6] (That is, the total product of progressively applying the generative rules for any one structure.) 'Any phrasemarker which meets these conditions *falls into the domain* of the transformation'. The idea of something happening in poetry in this sustained and systematic way – whenever a certain condition is fulfilled – is, I suppose, no part of our usual critical practice. We tend to think rather in terms of uniqueness and specificity. On reflection, there may be nothing in it to object to. Certain regularities, systematically sustained, are obviously present in verse: I mean, rhyme and metre. Why not others? Similarly with the idea that what is systematically present may be seen as a transformation. Once again this runs counter to received ideas. The poem, one wishes to maintain, is unparaphraseable. What is said in it cannot be said otherwise; how then can the text be understood as a re-writing of something else? Once more, the difficulty is apparent. One knows that most texts are in fact re-writings, transformations. They re-write what the poet last wrote, before he drafted the final version. No doubt a poet's transformations affect meaning as the linguist's do not. The whole point of conducting the enquiry in the more general terms now proposed, is to provide for just such discriminations.

My first example is so extremely simple that though I hope to show that a second example is significantly different from it, all

6. J. J. Katz and P. M. Postal, *An Integrated Theory of Linguistic Descriptions* (Cambridge, Mass., 1964), 9.

the same I am a little dubious about bringing it forward. It concerns the inversions from normal word-order in George Herbert's poem 'The Windows'. There are five in all, and they are marked in the text (below):

> Lord, how can man preach Thy eternal Word?
>   He is a brittle crazy glass,
> Yet in Thy temple Thou dost *him afford*
>   This glorious and transcendent place,
>   To be a window, through Thy grace.
>
> But when Thou dost anneal *in glass Thy story*,
>   Making Thy life to shine within
> The holy preachers, then the light and glory
>   *More reverend grows, and more doth win;*
>   Which else shows waterish, bleak, and thin.
>
> Doctrine and life, colours and light, *in one*
>   *When they combine* and mingle, bring
> A strong regard and awe; but speech alone
>   Doth vanish like a flaring thing,
>   And *in the ear, not conscience, ring*.

Obviously, poetic inversion like this may be seen as transformation, at least in a general sense, of a sentence having the standard order. 'He raised his head', say, would be the sentence 'generated' through the appropriate phrase-marker by the normal processes discussed by linguists; and 'His head he raised' would be a sort of optional poetic transformation of that, rather as 'Raised he his head (?)' would be the singular transformation (on an archaic model, needless to say) obligatory for the interrogative form. The transformations in Herbert's poem operate within what linguists call the 'verbal phrase', although they are not all of the same kind, and certainly they could not be subsumed under the linguist's technical requirements about analysability. The question is, whether one can suggest anything like a rule for these transformations: that is to say, a condition which, whenever fulfilled, will bring a transformation about.

Four of the five inversions obviously relate to the rhyme-scheme of the poem, and the fifth ('More reverend grows, and more doth win'), is what throws the parallel structure of this line into prominence (as is easily seen by 'de-naturing' it back to 'Grows more reverent and wins more'). In so doing, it helps the reader to take 'win' and 'grow' together, and so to understand better the full meaning of 'win': triumph, acquire, also persuade.

Here inversion seems to be related to a need to throw structure into relief. Where else is that need manifest? I think that, *in any poem*, one's answer might be: first, when the rhymes begin to come, and so the prosodic structure begins to take shape; next, when a new stanza begins, and so there is a need to bring out how the prosodic structure is repeating itself; and last, when the poem concludes, and the reader should therefore sense the completion of the structure.

In a three-stanza poem, this would give four places. Those are exactly the four places occupied by the rhyme-inversions in 'The Windows'. Add to this, the inversion in the line I discussed just now with a strongly marked internal and local structure,[7] and it becomes possible to say that all the inversions in this poem follow from a transformation-rule. The condition of the rule would be, that there exists a strong need – but a specifically *poetic* need – to emphasize metrical structure at a certain local point. When that condition is fulfilled, there comes an inversion of the word-order. The matter is a very simple one; but I find that something is learnt about the order and economy of this poem, by following it through.

I wish now to consider William Wordsworth's 'Anecdote for Fathers'.

> I have a boy of five years old;
> His face is fair and fresh to see;
> His limbs are cast in beauty's mould,
> And dearly he loves me.
>
> One morn we strolled on our dry walk,
> Our quiet home all full in view,
> And held such intermitted talk
> As we are wont to do.
>
> My thoughts on former pleasures ran;
> I thought of Kilve's delightful shore,
> Our pleasant home when spring began,
> A long, long year before.
>
> A day it was when I could bear
> Some fond regrets to entertain;
> With so much happiness to spare,
> I could not feel a pain.

7. If this could be said also of the last line, the inversion there would be serving a double purpose.

The green earth echoed to the feet
Of lambs that bounded through the glade,
From shade to sunshine, and as fleet
From sunshine back to shade.

Birds warbled round me – and each trace
Of inward sadness had its charm;
Kilve, thought I, was a favoured place,
And so is Liswyn farm.

My boy beside me tripped, so slim
And graceful in his rustic dress!
And, as we talked, I questioned him,
In very idleness.

'Now tell me, had you rather be'
I said, and took him by the arm,
'On Kilve's smooth shore, by the green sea,
Or here at Liswyn farm.'

In careless mood he looked at me,
While still I held him by the arm,
And said, 'At Kilve I'd rather be
Than here at Liswyn farm.'

'Now little Edward, say why so:
My little Edward, tell me why.' –
'I cannot tell, I do not know.' –
'Why, this is strange,' said I.

'For here are woods, hills smooth and warm:
There surely must some reason be
Why you would change sweet Liswyn farm
For Kilve by the green sea.'

At this the boy hung down his head,
He blushed with shame, nor made reply;
And three times to the child I said,
'Why, Edward, tell me why?'

His head he raised – there was in sight,
It caught his eye, he saw it plain –
Upon the house-top, glittering bright,
A broad and gilded vane.

Then did the boy his tongue unlock,
And eased his mind with this reply:
'At Kilve there was no weather-cock;
And that's the reason why.'

O dearest, dearest boy! my heart
For better lore would seldom yearn,
Could I but teach the hundredth part
Of what from thee I learn.

In this poem of sixty lines there are thirteen examples of inverted word-order. It seems self-evident that these inversions cannot be related to the prosodic structure in any way like that I suggested for Herbert's poem; and indeed, Wordsworth's simple and familiar metre, repeated fifteen times over, makes any such thing quite superfluous. Yet is there not a systematic correlation of another kind? Suppose one makes a list of the words running through the poem which express definite feelings, or clearly distinguishable intellectual operations. I think such a list would run 'loves'; 'pleasures'; 'delightful'; 'bear to entertain. . . regrets'; 'sadness'; – and so on. I should not include 'I questioned him in very idleness', because the verb here is qualified exactly so as to minimize the element of intellectual awareness; but 'my boy *tripped* beside me' and 'His head he raised . . . he saw it plain, it caught his eye', seem both to give emphatic expression to the emotional and mental life behind the physical action, and these I should indeed include. The lines which say that the poet asked the child 'Why?' three times over (stanza 12), also indicate a condition of mind wholly different from questioning in idleness. If one then tabulates the lines with these expressions, against those with inverted word-order, the result is as shown in table 7.

The correlation is remarkable. It justifies one's suggesting that in this poem, the inversions may also be thought of as resulting from a transformation-rule: though this time, the condition for the rule is the occurrence of what Coleridge called 'the best part of human language . . . derived from reflection on the arts of the mind itself', or, '. . . internal acts . . . processes and results of imagination'.[8]

Nor is the interest of these facts exhausted, when we have seen what might be called the principle of working of this particular poem. Wordsworth said little of what he meant when he spoke of trying to write in 'a *selection* of the language really used by men'; but what begins to show now, is how the selecting process took shape in his mind in this case. Strictly, of course, it is something

8. S. T. Coleridge, *Biographia Literaria*, ed. with an Introduction by G. Watson (London, 1956), 197.

Table 7

Wordsworth – anecdote for fathers
Here the columns represent the successive four line stanzas, and for each stanza the lines with strongly emotional or intellectual words or with inversions, are numbered, while the others are represented by dots.

Stanza	1	2	3	4	5	6	7	8
strongly emotional or intellectual words	...4	....	123.	1234	....	.23.	1...	....
inversions	...4	....	1...	12..	....	..3.	1...	....

Stanza	9	10	11	12	13	14	15
strongly emotional or intellectual words	1.3.	....	.2..	.23.	12..	12..	12.4
inversions	1.3.	....	.2..	..3.	1...	1...	.2.4

other than selection merely: emotion and intellectual activity do not induce a selection so much as a deviation from that language. One should note that the correlation throws up a genuine rule-situation. What we find is not the weak linkage that whenever there is inversion, emotion or intellectuality can be traced. It is the strong link, offering the beginnings of a genuine causal connection: almost whenever marked emotion or intellectuality is present the standard word-order is abandoned; and whenever it is not present, that order is maintained. Really this is an unexpected and I think noteworthy fact.

If we concede that there can be interest, in a poetic context, in the idea of a rule of transformation, even taken generally and not in the linguist's sense, then other poems seem to yield dividends in other ways. Herbert's 'Mortification' is an example. In the title, that word has its older meaning of being made to approach the state of death, as an exercise of virtue. The first stanza alone shows how exactly this epitomizes the structure of the poem:

> How soon doth man decay!
> When clothes are taken from a chest of sweets
> To swaddle infants, whose young breath
> Scarce knows the way,
> Those clouts are little winding-sheets,
> Which do consign and send them unto death.

When boys go first to bed,
They step into their voluntary graves:
    Sleep binds them fast; only their breath
        Makes them not dead.
    Successive nights, like rolling waves,
Convey them quickly who are bound for death.

        When youth is frank and free,
And calls for music, while his veins do swell,
    All day exchanging mirth and breath
        In company;
        That music summons to the knell
Which shall befriend him at the house of death.

        When man grows staid and wise,
Getting a house and home, where he may move
    Within the circle of his breath,
        Schooling his eyes;
        That dumb enclosure maketh love
Unto the coffin, that attends his death.

        When age grows low and weak,
Marking his grave, and thawing ev'ry year,
    Till all do melt, and drown his breath
        When he would speak;
    A chair or litter shows the bier
Which shall convey him to the house of death.

        Man, ere he is aware,
Hath put together a solemnity,
    And drest his hearse, while he has breath
        As yet to spare.
    Yet Lord, instruct us so to die
That all these dyings may be life in death.

Each of the first five stanzas follows a recurrent pattern. The boy's
bed is a grave; the young man's mirth and music summons him to
the in fact joy-bringing note of the funeral bell; the grown man's
family house 'maketh love with' – which I take to mean 'induces
love for' – the coffin; and the old man's 'chair or litter', which he
has to go about in, emblemizes ('shows') the bier that will take
him to the grave. The poem can be seen as the application, five
times over, of one and the same rule, which we should express as
something like 'whenever X stands for something in mortal life,
rewrite for X, X-plus-death'. Clothes + death = winding-sheet,
bed + death = grave, and so on. One sees how metaphor of this

kind has a wholly different nature from descriptive metaphor introduced for ornament or vividness.

If we think in this way we are helped to see not only the sharp organization of the poem, but also its limitations. On the one hand, this meticulous application (in effect) of a rewriting rule justifies, and at the same time is pointed out by, the 'breath-death' rhyme which is repeated through every stanza. The structure of the poem simply *is* to rewrite 'breath' as 'death' in various contexts. Yet even in seeing this exactness of structure, we surely sense something a little mechanically repetitive in it. So, perhaps, did Herbert. It is as if he were not quite satisfied merely to apply his transformation-rule stanza after stanza. Therefore, he related the 'breath' part of his figures, to the 'death' part, in no fewer than five different ways. It can be a relation of identity (stanzas 1 and 2); of emblematizing (stanza 5); of inviting cognition (stanza 3); or of inducing affection or love. I find these variations arbitrary and artificial, and they make me see the poem as a devout exercise more than anything else; though I can see how others might sense a welcome variety in a poem otherwise rather impaired by sameness.

In discussing Alexander Pope's translation of a short but celebrated passage from Homer, and along with it his pastiche of the same passage in *The Rape of the Lock*, I shall disregard how translation is itself systematic transformation. What transpires from examining the passages, is that further transformations, besides this primary one, are at work; and that they are not arbitrary, but systematic – and significant. Sarpedon's speech to Glaucon in the twelfth book of the *Iliad* (lines 322–8) runs:

> ὦ πέπον, εἰ μὲν γὰρ πόλεμον περὶ τόνδε φυγόντε
> αἰεὶ δὴ μέλλοιμεν ἀγήρω τ᾽ ἀθανάτω τε
> ἔσσεσθ᾽. οὔτε κεν αὐτὸς ἐνὶ πρώτοισι μαχοίμην
> οὔτε κε σε στέλλοιμι μάχην ἐς κυδιάνειραν
> νῦν δ᾽ ἔμπης γαρ κῆρες ἐφεστᾶσιν θανάτοιο
> μυρίαι, ἃς οὐκ ἔστι φυγεῖν βροτὸν οὐδ᾽ ὑπαλύξαι,
> ἴομεν, ἠέ τῳ εὖχος ὀρέξομεν, ἠέ τις ἡμῖν.

It is a typical passage of Homeric rhetoric, stately but terse, swift-moving, and strongly patterned. Antitheses run throughout: 'unageing. . . undying', in the second line, 'I should not fight myself. . . nor should I send you', in the third and fourth; 'not to flee, not to evade', in the sixth line, and 'either to give someone glory, or to have someone give it us', in the last and seventh. My prosaic translations, however, quite obscure the resonance of the original; and Pope's best-known predecessor, Chapman, who reproduced all the antitheses, did so in a loose, flexible pattern which obscured the resonance too. Pope's vision splendidly retains and renders that resonance; and one can identify two means whereby it does so. Here is what he wrote:

> Could all our care elude the gloomy grave,
> Which claims no less the fearful than the brave,
> For lust of fame I should not vainly dare
> In fighting fields, nor urge thy soul to war;
> But since, alas! ignoble age must come,
> Disease, and death's inexorable doom;
> The life which others pay, let us bestow,
> And give to fame what we to nature owe;
> Brave though we fall, and honoured if we live,
> Or let us glory gain, or glory give!

One soon sees how Pope retained what Chapman relinquished. Homer's four antitheses come successively in his second, third-fourth, and sixth and seventh lines. Pope renders these in his first, third-fourth, and sixth to tenth lines. These are the very lines which are strengthened by complex patterns of alliteration and assonance – I need only draw attention to the triple pattern in 'Could all our Care *elude* the *gloo*my Grave' and to the assonance concealed by spelling in '*o*thers pay – *u*s bestow'. Clearly these patterns contribute much to the effect; but they have nothing to do with transformations. They show however that Pope senses a purely local need for emphasis, where he notices what is locally emphatic in the original.

This justifies one in suggesting that he is also using another effect for the very same purpose. Pope closely reproduces the antitheses of the original by antitheses of his own. He cannot be said to translate 'unageing . . . undying' in Homer's second line at all, but he matches it. The second line of his translation: 'Which claims no less the *fearful* than the *brave*' throws into relief a sort of latent antithesis ('battle . . . fleeing') in the first line of the Homeric original. After that the matching is close: and whenever Pope presents his reader with an antithesis, he transforms the normal word-order to a poetic inversion (lines 2, 3, 7–8, 10). Once again, thinking of the passage of verse as somehow systematically controlled by a transformation-rule governed by a determinate condition throws significant light. 'Poetic' inversion turns out to be no mere mannerism; and also, of course, no mere prosodic convenience. It is a substantial device, systematically in service, to make sharp and conspicuous what the poetic qualities of the original require should be so.

The pastiche in *The Rape of the Lock* (a pastiche related of course to Homer's lines, not to Pope's translation) raises issues of another kind.

> Oh! if to dance all Night, and dress all Day,
> Charm'd the Small-pox, or chas'd old Age away;
> Who would not scorn what Huswife's Cares produce,
> Or who would learn one earthly Thing of Use?
> To patch, nay ogle, might become a Saint,
> Nor could it sure be such a Sin to paint.
> But since, alas! frail Beauty must decay,
> Curl'd or uncurl'd, since Locks will turn to grey,
> Since painted, or not painted, all shall fade,
> And she who scorns a Man, must die a Maid;
> What then remains, but well our Pow'r to use,
> And keep good Humour still whate'er we lose?
> And trust me, Dear! good Humour can prevail,
> When Airs, and Flights, and Screams, and Scolding fail.
> Beauties in vain their pretty Eyes may roll;
> Charms strike the Sight, but Merit wins the Soul.

Sixteen lines in length, this pastiche is a substantial expansion of the original. Even so, it contains only two examples of inverted word-order (lines 11, 15) and there is nothing important to make of them. To begin with, rather, the pastiche effect can be thought of as structurally like that operating in Herbert's 'Mortification'. In content, as opposed to structure, it is of course entirely different. In view of the *locale* of Pope's poem, we could, facetiously, write it out as a transformation like this:

> Homer → Homer + *Hampton*

'Fighting among the foremost' becomes the 'huswife's cares'. 'Glory' becomes 'good-humour', and so on.

Yet this is not the whole story. There is something else which, throughout the passage, Pope does in a regular, a rule-like way. Homer, at least until his last line, does more (as is natural in a tragic passage) to point out the harsh realities of man's life than its (illusory) compensations: 'the battle'; 'fight among the foremost';

'the fight that brings us honour'; 'the ten thousand tribulations of death'. Twice there comes the thought of uselessly fleeing. In his translation, Pope was abundantly to preserve these proportions. But in *The Rape of the Lock* it is otherwise: they would have destroyed the decorum of the lighter poem. The result is, that whenever the note of the original is too solemn for his purposes, Pope inconspicuously modifies it. Partly, he does this simply through the 'Homer → Homer + Hampton' rule, which mitigates 'death' (Homer, line 2) to old age, and old age to small-pox. But by itself, this would not be enough. We should still have too much, in the end, of 'grave Clarissa'. So, in part, it is done also by another transformation: writing about what is or might be fled *to*, instead of what is fled *from*. 'fleeing from the *battle*' becomes 'to dance all night, and dress all day'. The 'tribulations of *death* are myriad' becomes '*beauty* must decay'. The nearest Pope comes to 'one may not flee mortality, one may not evade it' is his reference to the locks – the Lock of the poem comes to mind of course – 'curl'd, or uncurl'd'. This, notice, is not one among a variety of devices used at random. It is the recurrent method, in addition to the primary, 'Homer + Hampton' transformation, which Pope relies upon to shift the tone of his verse, because it shifts the apparent pre-occupation of the passage. Moreover, it receives an extension in the two passages which are out and out additions: the 'To patch, nay ogle' complex and the last five lines. In these interpolations – they are purely that – Pope maintains the necessary lightness of tone, by amplifying the very thing – the Hampton and Belinda world – which the passage as a whole condemns and rejects; and which, as it were, it derives authority to reject from the Homeric original.

What I am claiming is this. Simply by general analogy with the linguists' mode of thought, we can study Pope's two passages, the translation as well as the pastiche, as constructed by systematic application of rules of transformation. For the version in Pope's 'Homer' itself, the rules would be, first, the general rule of translation, and then an inversion-with-antithesis rule. For the pastiche the rules would be, first, I suppose, the translation transformation, though that of course becomes largely or wholly overlaid; second, the pastiche, 'Homer + Hampton' transformation; and third, a transformation which I think may be put like this. Pope is as if writing by a rule whereby under certain conditions, a sentence about the *positive* of the satire (the world, that is, of 'good-humour' – and of the cares and utilities of life) is replaced by one about the *target* of the satire (dancing all night, etc.). It seems to me that, modestly no doubt, the organization, edge and effectiveness of both passages are clarified by this way of thinking about them.

My last example is too long to quote at length or discuss in full, but doubtless it has the advantage of being familiar to all. It is the death of Antony scene in *Antony and Cleopatra*: Act IV, scene xv, line 9 to the end. In an earlier play Troilus bade farewell to Cressida – he did most of the talking – in a diction that was leisurely and loftily sustained.

> We two, that with so many thousand sighs
> Did buy each other, must poorly sell ourselves
> With the rude brevity and discharge of one.

Simply to look at that speech of Troilus is to have the discontinuities of the *Antony and Cleopatra* scene thrust on the attention. On the one hand, there is Cleopatra's:

> O sun
> Burn the great sphere thou mov'st in . . .

or Antony's:

> – please your thoughts
> In feeding them with those my former fortunes
> Wherein I liv'd the greatest prince o' th' world,
> The noblest . . .

Splendid rhetoric, courtly oratory. On the other hand Cleopatra's:

> – the maid that milks
> And does the meanest chares.

Antony never adopts quite this homely simplicity, but once – and the contrast with Troilus's style is eloquent – he seems almost deliberately to transform his way of speaking from the oratorical into a kind of gentle plainness:

> I here importune death awhile, until
> Of many thousand kisses *the poor last*
> *I lay upon thy lips*

I referred – of set purpose – to Antony's 'transforming' how he spoke. Suppose we tried to identify something like a 'standard' of diction for Antony and for Cleopatra: how Shakespeare makes them speak when he wishes to convey that they are being their ordinary selves, neither acting out a *rôle* nor under stress of emotion. We might, for Antony, take what he says to Enobarbus in II.iii:

> No more light answers. Let our officers
> Have notice what we purpose. I shall break
> The cause of our expedience to the Queen,
> And get her leave to part . . .

– dignified, but plain, terse, to the point. For Cleopatra, there is her speech to Charmian in I.v:

> He was not sad, for he would shine on those
> That make their looks by his; he was not merry,
> Which seem'd to tell them his remembrance lay
> In Egypt with his joy; but between both.

– more animated, doubtless, but perhaps also acceptable as a standard. Given these two standards, the discontinuities of the death-scene could be seen as resulting from the working out of two transformation-processes: one, as it were a re-writing upwards towards rhetoric, and the other a re-writing downwards towards a kind of the ultimate simplicity. But a transformation-process is one thing, and the operation of a transformation-*rule* another. For that – we may recall how the point was expressed by Katz and Postal – the case must 'meet conditions' which bring it about that the utterance 'falls into the domain of the transformation'.

To an astonishing degree – one cannot say less – the necessary conditions may be traced throughout this scene. They are not matters open to esoteric poetic sensibility alone, but show in the elementary structuring of the dialogue. Briefly, if somewhat irreverently, what happens may be put like this. When either character utters a sentence about Cleopatra, there is a re-writing downwards, into the tragic plain style. When either speaks about any other character (save for two references to Octavius, and one to Octavia, it is always Antony himself) there is a re-writing upwards into one or another kind of rhetoric. Cleopatra's line:

> Here's sport indeed! How heavy weighs my lord!

is an apparent exception only, once we see that the first words are spoken in toilsome self-preoccupation, while the rest recalls an Antony momentarily half-forgotten.

The one real exception comes at the end, and I think that the present mode of analysis throws its importance into sharp relief. Cleopatra says:

> We'll bury him: *and then*, what's brave, what's noble,
> Let's do it after the high Roman fashion,
> And make death proud to take us.

The words 'and then' are the clue. When Cleopatra faces the thought of Antony's final disappearance from her life, there is a moment not merely of stylistic, but of major dramatic transformation, and she recalls herself once more as an autonomous public figure and a monarch. But what makes this sudden change readily available to us through a mere nuance of style, is the firm linguistic structure that has preceded it throughout. In fact, Cleopatra's two women have already pointed to that structure, as in their contrasting ways they try to revive Cleopatra when she swoons:

> Charmian: O madam, madam, madam!
> Iras: *Royal Egypt, Empress!*

In a word: once Cleopatra thinks of Antony as buried, she can hear the voice of Iras again.

The critic, I venture to suggest, should be a little above simply 'borrowing techniques' from the linguist. Quite possibly, this borrowing might give lucky results from time to time: but for preference he should leave work to others, and one must add that its successes have been few and partial. What it falls to the critic to do is, rather, to contemplate certain fundamental conceptions which he finds in other disciplines, and suspects might somehow prove fertile in his own; and then, to fall to work with them, once they have taken a shape in his mind which he believes to be genuinely adapted to his unique material and the unique problems which he pursues in respect of it. That is what I have tried to do, though I know it is the merest beginning.

Logic, feeling and structure in
nineteenth-century political oratory: a primer
of analysis

I

1.0 This essay proposes:

i. to identify and elucidate some of the things in certain parliamentary or public oratory of the nineteenth century which to a
greater or lesser extent endow it with literary quality, and cause it
to invite a response such as is given to examples of the literary art.

ii. from findings under (i), in certain respects to posit for review
the general nature of a literary work.

2.0 Is the most conspicuous and perhaps distinguishing quality of
the oratorical work, *eloquence?* 'Eloquence', insofar as that word
has loose association with 'rhetoric' (modern, broad sense) and
'oratory', is well understood: at least, well enough for present
limited purposes. 'Eloquence', so understood, is what Dickens
satirized in Mr Serjeant Buzfuz. It can be defined in intention.
Probably it can be identified and determined only in extension (as
with other terms for special language, like 'vernacular', 'poetic
diction', etc.). That is to say, reference must ultimately be to a
historically specific list of eloquence-structures, and the
eloquence-terms that can complete them.

2.1 The Copernican Revolution occurs in the literary study of
oratory when eloquence is recognized as a side issue. It is not the
achievement but the convention of oratory. Statements 2.2
and 2.3 propose parallel cases which help to bring this out. In
the interests of brevity, they are related to local literary quality
only.

2.2 While literary quality in Pope's verse, or Johnson's, was seen
as in a category such as 'perfection of the couplet', convention was
mistaken for achievement. Today the virtual starting-point for
analysis of literary quality as locally manifested in their verse

would be verbal texture, figurative structure, quality of statement, argument structure, etc.

2.3 The argument of 2.2 applies to the verse of Shelley, Keats, or Tennyson viewed in terms of a category like 'music'.

2.4 In all cases, there will be an initial achievement (which may be called the achievement of competence) simply in sustained conformity to the chosen convention. Decisive achievement will lie in the creation, within the convention, of a reality which invites apprehension through one or other of the fundamental literary modes.

2.5 The assertion in 2.4 is argued for, in respect of the present subject, to the degree that the remainder of this essay identifies, within the oratorical work, achievement in one or other of the fundamental literary modes. This is its major purpose. To say that achievement is in a fundamental mode *is to say* that it excels any achievement of competence.

3.0 Form is among the fundamental modes.

3.01 Statement 3.0 does not define its subject-term.

3.1 A literary work may be endowed with form in more ways than one. In the present context (but see 12.5), nothing is being said against views such as that form is characteristically, regularly, always, or best generated through the creation of value structures, or the posing, stressing, pondering, wrestling with, or solution of questions, problems, issues, and so on. I note this to avoid confusion with views I have expressed elsewhere.[1] The present argument requires, however, the postulates listed in 3.2 and 3.3.

3.2 *Certain general postulates of criticism*

P_1 Self-consistency is *prima facie* a desirable quality in a work of literary art. (Note: for 'prima facie', 'necessarily' may be read if wished.)

P_2 It is standard critical practice to *propound* causal connections between a given emotional-imaginative response and a 'feature' which the critic connects with that in interpretation, and not to prove their existence after the manner of a scientist.

P_3 Literary apprehension is not confined to what the text expresses explicitly and overtly.

1. e.g. in *The Story of the Night* (1961), pp. 1–20.

P_4 In literary works of certain major types (drama, novel, etc.), imaginative form is regularly related to developing patterns of sympathy and antipathy for individual characters.

P_5 In literary works of perhaps all types, imaginative form is regularly related to developing patterns of endorsement or non-endorsement of entities which may at least to a limited extent be formulated as propositions.

> *Lemma to P_5*: P_4 may or may not be reducible to P_5.

P_6 Every literary work has a 'theme' (or themes) which is embodied in its details. (N.B. This is a conventional postulate: it is probably reducible to P_5.)

3.3 Axioms of the criticism of oratory

A_1 Literary form is not identical in quality with, nor apprehended in the same way as, logical form. This axiom will be accepted on inspection of complexes having *either* literary *or* logical form, but not both.

A_2 Literary form is characteristically related to sequential order. This axiom will be accepted on inspection of complexes having literary form, alongside complexes composed of the same parts (stanzas, lines, sentences, etc.) re-arranged in another sequential order; when it will be found that characteristically the form is changed.

> *Lemma 1 to A_2*. In principle, re-arrangement may *improve* literary form: that this could not be so of logical form, and moreover that re-arrangement of the parts of a complex having logical form is properly speaking not re-arrangement but dis-arrangement are necessary propositions.
>
> *Lemma 2 to A_2*: Lemma 1 to A_2 may be used to elucidate A_1 if required.

4.0 The work of oratory may have literary form, distinguishable from its logical form (its argument structure) and illustrative of A_1 and A_2.

5.0 EXAMPLE ONE of 4.0 the first oratical work proposed for detailed examination is (A) *George Canning, Speech on Parliamentary Reform Given at a Public Dinner in Liverpool, 18 March 1820.*[2] Polemics of this kind are often impressive for sustained and

---

2. George Canning, *Speeches*, 6 vols, London, 1828, VI, 369–93.

versatile covert denigration of the speaker's opponents. This denigration can rise to the level of notable verbal dexterity and command of language, though to speak in this way is in itself to imply that it is barely among the fundamental modes of literary achievement. But I find very little of such insinuation and innuendo in *A*. Again, in the closing pages of the present essay, there is a brief review of the literary impact of sustained interaction of the general and the particular in works of oratory. Canning's dependence, in general, on something like a Burkeian conception of the state is plain enough in *A*, but that dependence is of a straightforward and indeed rather pedestrian, kind; and is also not fully self-consistent. Therefore, (by 3.2, P_1) nothing has been done so far to establish *A* as a work of literary art.

5.1 Nevertheless, *A* unquestionably strikes the reader, on reflection, as having some great persuasive quality which is intangible, and barely related to the cogency of the speech as a piece of argument. It seems to have some almost poetic power to convince, and to invite response by what must be called the literary imagination.

5.2 *I propound*, as cause of this (refer to 3.2, P_2), a *basic rhythm of alternation* which may be traced almost throughout the speech. This alternating pattern is between two generic ideas. They take many different local forms, varying with the immediate context; they alternate almost continuously throughout, regardless of whether they themselves are under discussion or not; and they enact, but do not necessarily state, Canning's fundamental ideas on his subject. (Therefore see 3.2, P_3.) Speaking loosely, the effect is a little like that of a *passacaglia* in music.

5.3 Canning is opposed to general parliamentary reform of the kind under discussion in 1820. He sees it as likely to bring only pervasive unrest and disorder. The two alternating ideas are (A) destructive and disastrous activity and movement and (B) the stable, the static, the orderly.

5.4 In 5.5 an attempt is made to sketch this complex structure, on a manageable scale, diagrammatically. Page references are given, followed by decimal points that divide the page by eye into tenths (thus 369.7 means seven-tenths of the way down page 369). Even without reference to the full text, these bring out the virtual continuity of the alternation. This brings out in its turn the fact that the fundamental choice Canning wishes his audience to see

and to make is implicitly present to them by enactment, regardless of what is for the time being under explicit discussion (3.2,
P_3). The table sets out the alternation in two columns. Two
remarks in the speech, conspicuously *inviting attention to a developing contrast*, are centered and italicized in the schema below. So is
the opening paragraph, which does the same. Three such invi-
tations are a significant recurrence. But it should be noted that the
speech does not begin by discussing the general question of
reform at all. What Canning has to say on that subject is already
transpiring, by the *passacaglia* enactment, while he deals with
things of much more limited scope.

5.5 *Illustrative scheme for 5.4*

(GENERIC IDEA OF TYPE A)   (GENERIC IDEA OF TYPE B)

*Part I: Defence of the recently imposed restrictions on public
meetings (the 'Six Acts', 1820)*

Opening Paragraph

> Gentlemen, short as is the interval
> since I last met you in this place on a
> similar occasion, the events which have
> filled up that interval have not been
> unimportant. The great moral disease
> which we then talked of as gaining
> ground on the community has, since
> that period, arrived at its most
> extravagant height; and, since that
> period also, remedies have been
> applied to it, if not of permanent cure,
> at least of temporary mitigation.

TYPE A	TYPE B
	370.7 *whether any country . . . ever presented such a contrast.*
371 Crown in danger . . . anxiety and dismay . . . irresistible diffusion of doctrines hostile to the very existence of Parliament	
	372.5 tendency to root the attachment to monarchy deeper in the hearts of the people

TYPE A	TYPE B
	372.6 restoration of peace throughout the country
373.3 menace . . . charge (i.e. accusation)	
	373.4 answered [by Canning's own overwhelming majority in his own constituency]
	373.6 British liberty was established [Note: Canning means long *before* the Gordon Riots, not as their immediate sequel]
374.2 Lord George Gordon [of the 'Gordon Riots'] . . . demolition of chapels and dwelling-houses, the breaking of prisons and the conflagration of London	
374.9 countless multitudes . . . without reference to the comfort . . . of the neighbourhood	
	375.2 I have a right to quiet in my house . . . I call upon the laws
375.7 turbulent . . . tumult	
	375.8 orderly meeting
376.3 multitudes . . . irresponsible . . . caprice	
	376.5 . . . a spirit of corporation
376.5 . . . *the spirit of the laws goes directly the other way*	
377.3 collect a mob . . . set half Manchester on fire . . . French Revolution	
	377.8 the law prescribes a corporate character
378.5 a multitude . . . no common tie . . . wrought up to mischief	
	378.7 How different are the genuine and recognized modes of ascertaining national opinion
378.8 untold multitudes	

TYPE A	TYPE B
	378.8 No! corporations in their corporate capacity . . . recognized bodies of the state
379.3 tyranny . . . despot . . . mob . . . inflamed and infuriated population . . . reign of terror	
	379.9 responsibility
379.9 degrade into multitudes . . . what security have you . . .	
	380.5 lawful authority . . . respectable community . . . authority

Part II: Argument against radical electoral reform

TYPE A	TYPE B
384.5 sweep away 385.6 . . . the leap is taken . . . did not stop there 386.5 in a few weeks the House of Peers was voted useless. We all know what happened to the Crown (i.e. in the 1640s)	
	387.3 I for my part will not consent to take one step . . .
389.8 again destroy . . . dispossess	
	391.8 . . . I fear to touch that balance
392.6 brink of a precipice . . . fall . . . hurry . . . irretrievable destruction	
	392.9 stake in the country . . . Government under which he lives . . . steadfastly

5.6 For clarity, 5.6 recapitulates 5.2.

6.0 EXAMPLE TWO of 4.0. The second oratorical work proposed for detailed examination is (B) *Robert Lowe, Speech in the House of Commons, 26 April 1866, on the Second Reading of the Representation of the People Bill*[3]. B is perhaps Lowe's most celebrated speech, as *A* is Canning's. What is now to be discussed is its claim to distinctively literary status as under 3.0.

6.1 Literary form (refer to 3.3, and for the purpose of the present paragraph to 3.2, P_2) is manifested in *B* not as a rhythm of alternation, but insofar as (1) by its organization of material and (2) by its changing tone, it enacts and embodies, from beginning through to end, the sort of development which its speaker envisages over future history if the House passes the measure to which he is opposed. (Page-decimals are used as before.)

6.2 *Organization of material*

Lowe asserts that the principle of the Bill has not been stated by its proponents. It may be (I) that the franchise ought to be given to *all* those who in themselves are fitted for it; this would then be done as an end in itself. Or (II) that the franchise ought to be given *only* to those to whom giving it is a means to ends other than itself (viz., good government, as defined on p. 105.3). The main argument of the speech opens when Lowe asserts ('and so the thing comes round again': p. 126.9) that the Bill is based on I, and that this false principle must inevitably open the floodgates and bring national destruction.

6.3 Thenceforth, the material of the speech has an organization that enacts this kind of process. Lowe opened with a topic – the semantic distinction between one formulation of principle and another – which invites and indeed demands the sharpest focusing of attention. Progressively, throughout the whole work, the attention of reader/audience is extended more widely. The principle of the Bill, Lowe first notes, is admitted by his opponents (p. 125) to call for the enfranchisement of the whole working class. His opponents talk merely of a difference of one pound sterling; the reality behind that is on another scale: 100,000 men (p. 128). Moreover, universal education requires to be surveyed, not universal enfranchisement alone (p. 136). Beyond that, it is necessary to look back to 1848, the year of Revolutions; to take into account the teachings of Fourier and Saint-Simon (p. 138) and the trades union movement and its restrictive practices – as these are noted in Birmingham, say, or Edinburgh (p. 140); or to look to France and America 'where Democracy may be said to have run its

3. Robert Lowe, *Speeches and Letters on Reform*, London, 1867, pp. 102–70.

course and arrived at something like its ultimate limits' (p. 146);
or to the 'terrible . . . power' of Democracy for war (the Ameri-
can Civil War), and then to the Crimea, Turkey, Hungary in 1849.
Poland, the Australian colonies, Canada (p. 149). The whole line
of thought must lead to the end of the House of Peers – the
Church – the Judiciary – the Commons itself – probably the
Throne. But finally: we learn better if we survey 'history' and 'the
stream of time' (p. 168) – going back to Virgil and the sack of
Troy, or the Book of Judges. After the Book of Judges, only
seventeen words remain of a speech of seventeen thousand.

6.4 *Tone*

Gathering acerbity of tone is a common practice in oratory: its
presence in *B* is noted briefly as a second embodiment, in texture
and implicitly, of the developing non-logical structure. The following quotations sketch out the appropriate schema:

> *page*
> 102 'it is not inopportune to ask'
> 'rather pale and colourless' [N.B. This is said of his opponents'
> views: as *assertion* the phrase sharpens tone, but merely as
> *diction*, its tendency is to mollify it.]
> 131 'why shouldn't we call it by its right name at once?'
> 132 'the member for Westminster has come out in a new character'
> 140 'no one can tell where it will stop' [i.e. the destructive move-
> ment of events, once it sets in]
> 142 'like men contending with a maelstrom into which . . . eventu-
> ally they will be sucked'
> 157 'absolutely tramples down'

(closing sentence) 'History may tell of other acts as signally disastrous,
but of none more wanton, none more disgraceful'.

By the end of the speech, Lowe's rhythms (e.g., the superb
sentence just quoted) enact his thought, and so does the final
image: 'we are about to pluck down on our own heads the
venerable temple of our liberty and glory.' What can be, at one
and the same moment, both Samson and the whole host of the
Philistines? Only 'the Multitude united in one Person . . . that
great Leviathan or rather (to speak more reverently) that *Mortall
God*'. Lowe's term for the Hobbesian state is 'Caesarianism', and
on p. 163 of the text he envisages its coming.

6.5 Recapitulates, for clarity, 6.1.

II

7.0 P_4 (3.2) regularly has its analogue in the oratorical work.

7.01 the patterns referred to in 7.0 regularly develop as between the speaker *and his opponent.*

7.02 These patterns develop in the course of manipulated argument. They are therefore related to logic, and it is a differentiating aspect of the literary quality of the oratorical work that its analogue to P_4 so develops. For these reasons it is both possible, and desirable, to formalize such patterns in a rudimentary notation. But if these patterns were patterns of true/false or agreement/disagreement only, they would not present an analogue to P_4. Therefore their expression in a notation requires symbols additional to those employed in the logic of implication. In fact, the notation now to be proposed differs essentially in function from that of implication logic.

7.1 Argument and criticism of argument create patterns of emotional response in the audience and in respect of, especially, the speaker's opponent(s). If the following analyses demonstrate this, then 7.0 is valid, and the discussion is relevant to the purpose enunciated in 2.5.

7.2 *The Notation (I)*

Df

The following are definitions (=):

Df
$S[p]$ = the speaker believes proposition p.[4]
Df
$O[p]$ = the speaker's opponent believes proposition p.

I employ p, q, etc., for propositions in general, but in the worked examples these are replaced by Roman numerals (I, II, etc.) which represent, as shown in each case afresh, actual and particular statements paraphrased from the texts. Since I, II, etc., are semantically determinate, it is sometimes useful to employ $\frac{c}{p}$ or $\frac{c}{I}$ to mean 'the logical converse of p (or I)'. Thus p, q, S $[p]$ and O $[p]$ represent typical propositions in the notation. In addition to these symbols, brackets, the signs ~ (not), ∨ (or), · (and), and occasion-

---

4. Contrast Jaakko Hintikka's notation, B_{ap} (*Knowledge and Belief*, Cornell, 1962). But relegation of the believer to a subscript is not helpful in the present context.

ally the modifications of · to substitute for brackets (i.e. : , : ·) are employed as in the logic of implication. It should be noted that →, where it occurs, is a genuinely semantic relation when it relates the Roman numerals: i.e. I → II may be seen to be true or false from the meanings of I and II as given in the paraphrases. 'Establishes' is a better term for it than 'entails', because what it frequently (though not always) represents is a probable argument.

7.3 *The Notation (II): emotion symbols* (see 7.02)
The following are definitions:

$$\underset{\text{Df}}{\approx} p = p \text{ is a ridiculous or disreputable proposition}$$

$$\underset{\text{Df}}{\downarrow} O = O \text{ is discredited}$$

The sign ! is used to mark the termination of an argument in a discrediting. It should be noted that $\sim (\approx p \cdot = \cdot \sim \sim p)$, although $\approx p$ often corresponds approximately to the expression 'doubly false' (therefore self-evidently false to those not blinded by stupidity or prejudice).

This is why the commonest form of argument is probably:

$$\approx p \cdot O\, [p] \cdot \rightarrow \cdot \downarrow O !$$

p could sometimes be expressed in notation:

$$\approx p \cdot = \cdot p \rightarrow q \cdot \sim (q \rightarrow p) \cdot \sim q$$

meaning something like 'even the implications of p, weaker than itself, are false'. E.g. 'All members of the U.S. Republican Party are Communist' is a ridiculous proposition, since not even any sub-class of the Republican Party is Communist (or so I believe). The force of $\approx p$ in certain arguments seems to be best brought out by subsequently duplicating the other emotion symbol, or the 'argues for' sign. Thus:

$$\approx p \cdot O\,[p] \cdot \rightarrow \cdot \downarrow \downarrow O !$$
$$\text{or } \approx p \cdot O\,[p] \cdot \underset{\rightarrow}{\rightarrow} \cdot \downarrow O ! \text{ ('one cannot possibly escape the conclusion that . . .')}$$

7.4
It is no part of the present essay's purpose to construct a calculus in the notation. Nevertheless, it may be the case that this can be done, since it seems clear that certain propositions could be taken as primitive. E.g.:

(i) $\sim p \cdot O\,[p] \cdot \rightarrow \cdot \downarrow O\,!$
  (Whoever believes a false proposition is discredited.)

(ii) $O\,[p] \cdot p \rightarrow q \cdot \rightarrow \cdot O\,[q] \vee \downarrow O\,!$
  (Whoever does not believe, or disbelieves, the implications of what he believes, is discredited.)

(iii) $O\,[p] \cdot O\,[\sim p] \cdot \rightarrow \cdot \downarrow O\,!$
  (Whoever believes a self-contradiction is discredited; but this presumably follows from $\approx p \cdot O\,[p] \cdot \rightarrow \cdot \downarrow O\,!$, since all self-contradictions are ridiculous propositions.)

7.5 EXAMPLE ONE of 7.01. The first speech analysed is (C) *W. E. Gladstone, Speech on Moving the Second Reading of the Representation of the People Bill, 12 April 1866*.[5] This speech contains (among much else, of course) the following argument: First, (I) the working classes make a full contribution (through taxation, which is based directly or indirectly on income) to the expenses of government. Therefore, (II) the working classes should contribute correspondingly, through the franchise, to the constitution of government in the House of Commons. But it may be said that (III) property and not income is the correct basis on which to assess eligibility for the franchise. (Some Opposition members were obliging and incautious enough to cry 'Hear, hear!' at this point.) But if so, one must 'take the consequence' (p. 107.8). It is that (IV) property should provide thirteen-fourteenths of the national budget, instead of income as at present. Since it is clear that to advocate IV was in no way part of Gladstone's purpose, one can see already that something other than a proposition is the 'target' of the argument. That something is O.

7.6 There are two implicit premises in Gladstone's own position, which is, of course, I → II. The first premise is (V) participation in the expenses of government qualifies a man for enfranchisement. (This is simply 'No taxation without representation'.) The second is the logical converse of V; or more precisely perhaps, $\approx \left(\sim \frac{c}{V} \right)$, i.e. the denial of 'no representation without paying some tax' is a disreputable proposition.

7.7 The argument paraphrased in 7.5 may now be expressed in notation as follows:

  a. $O\,[V] : I \cdot V \cdot \rightarrow \cdot II$ (All British politicians in 1866 must [V])
  b. $O\,[\sim I] \cdot O\,[III]$ (By the debate, and the cries of 'Hear, hear!')

5. W. E. Gladstone, *Speeches on Parliamentary Reform in 1866*, London, 1866, pp. 91–130.

c. but III $\rightarrow$ IV $\cdot$ V $\cdot$ $\sim\frac{c}{V}$ ('if $\sim$ [III $\rightarrow$ IV], it could be just to have a vote and pay no taxes')

d. therefore O [IV] $\cdot$ V $\cdot$ O$\left[\sim\frac{c}{V}\right]$

e. but O [$\sim$ IV]$\approx\left(\sim\frac{c}{V}\right)$ ('it could be just . . . (etc.)' is a disreputable proposition)

f. therefore: O [IV $\cdot$ $\sim$ IV] $\cdot$ V $\cdot$ O$\left[\sim\frac{c}{V}\right]\cdot\approx\left[\sim\frac{c}{V}\right]: \rightarrow\,:\downarrow$O !

That is to say, Gladstone's opponents are discredited by believing either a self-contradictory proposition or a disreputable one.

8.0 EXAMPLE TWO of 7.01. In the same speech occurs the following rebuttal of opponents' argument. (Note that in each example worked the Roman numerals take fresh meanings.) Those opponents assert that (I) where the working class has a majority it will vote as a class. But (II) 'municipal franchises are in a predominant degree working men's franchises', and (III) municipal elections are not fought on a class basis. Moreover, (IV) Parliamentary borough constituencies in which there are already working-class majorities now return more Opposition (i.e. Conservative) than Gladstonian (Liberal) members.

8.1 There is again an implicit premise, treated as axiomatic: it is that (V) a working-class majority could not return a Conservative MP if it voted on a class basis. The argument may then be expressed in notation:

a. II $\cdot$ III : II $\cdot$ III $\cdot\rightarrow\cdot$ $\sim$ I (the true propositions II and III disprove I)

b. IV $\cdot$ V : IV $\cdot$ V $\cdot\rightarrow\cdot$ $\sim$ I (the true propositions IV and V independently do the same)

c. therefore $\approx$I

d. but O [I]

e. O [I] $\cdot\approx$I $\cdot\rightarrow\cdot\downarrow$O !

That I is a ridiculous proposition, not merely a false one, transpires in the text (p. 108.3): 'is there any shade of shadow, any rag, even, of proof . . . ?' The question is rhetorical. The depreciatory force of the conclusion is especially clear from *b* above, in that Gladstone's opponents know *only too well* that these propositions are true: IV is to their most immediate advantage, V follows from their very identity. (Note: a modern reader is likely, perhaps, to understand V too strongly and therefore to see IV as itself beginning to discredit Conservative MPs, at least those so elected. But there is nothing of this in the speech: one must remember that neither Gladstone nor his opponents would have called them-selves democrats or said that they advocated democracy. Glad-stone's position would certainly have been that a Conservative member did not represent the true interest of a working class electing him, *only* because as a Conservative he did not represent the true interest of the country. Neither side saw class interests as they are widely seen now.)

8.2 It should be noted that in the full text (p. 111), the paragraph, expressing IV · V · → · ∼ I (i.e. b in 8.1) closes by putting the idea of 'the Opposition' before the reader/audience as emphatically as it possibly can. Once more, it is the implication of the train of thought in respect of them, not merely of a proposition, which is the nerve of it.

9.0 EXAMPLE THREE of 7.01. 'Sir, I must now beg leave to deny' that (I) '. . . (a) general transfer of power, either in counties or boroughs, is contemplated by this Bill' (p. 118). This conclusion is valid because (II) majorities determine results (this means, a majority of a certain class elects a candidate to serve that class: O [II] *from proposition I of the last example*); and (III) there are no county constituencies in which the working class have a majority. But furthermore, (IV) they will have a majority only in fewer than half of the boroughs, even when the Bill passes. But, Glad-stone says, if his opponents stress the influence of the working class in the counties, despite their minority position, 'I shall be obliged to put the proposition in a manner much more unfavour-able to my opponents' (p. 120). It would then be proper to stress middle- and upper-class influence where those classes, in their turn, do not command a majority: all the more so, in fact, since wealth and position are intrinsically more influential than the lack of those things.

9.1 Depreciation of the opponents, in contrast to argument sim-ply against a proposition, is plain here not only from the last quotation (9.0), but also from Gladstone's opening words: 'We are met too much . . . not by reasoning, but by suspicions and fears'. The notation, as before, brings out how intimately depre-ciation is involved with the logical structure:

    a. III · IV ·→∼ I ∨ ∼ II
    b. O [I]
    c. therefore, O [∼ II] ∨ O [I ∼ I] (from which ↓ O !)
    d. but ∼ II → ∼ I (if majorities do not determine results, it follows

without more ado that not even a working-class majority is
necessarily going to bring in its own candidate)

e. moreover, I → II (this should be taken semantically; but it
follows from $p \rightarrow q \cdot \rightarrow \cdot \sim q \rightarrow \sim p$ in the logic of implication)

f. therefore, O [I ∼ I · II ∼ II] from which ↓↓O !

Gladstone's opponents commit themselves to two self-
contradictions: clear evidence for the quotation above ('We are
met . . .').

10.0 The purpose of the discussion from 7.0 may now be recalled.
It has been to show that the oratorical texture carries a constant,
and indeed (review the page references) not far short of continuous, creation of patterns of thought culminating in *depreciation and
negative feeling-response (antipathy) for the speaker's opponent*; and
therefore, by implication, approval and sympathy for the speaker.
There is, we may say, a more or less permanent texture *of dramatization and characterization*. Then see 3.2, P_4, and 2.5.

10.1 The occurrence of these patterns, at least here and there in a
text, could have been demonstrated merely by quoting disparag-
ing or ironical references to opponents which occur from time to
time. Why then the notation? Because such evidence would have
been evidence of *intermittent and non-essential* dramatization and
characterization. The notation, however, shows succinctly that
these are intrinsic to structure because they are set up by the logic
itself of one argument after another. Remove that from which
they of necessity result and the oratorical work disappears as a
whole. That the polemical activity, insofar as it is conducted by
argument and the rebuttal of argument, creates patterns is a
necessary and not a contingent proposition. Thus the notation
brings out how the analogue of the oratorical work to the
literary-imaginative one, under P_4, is not intermittent but pervasive, and not incidental but carried by its structure and therefore
characteristic. Refer then to 4.0 and 3.0.

11.0 P_5 regularly has its analogue in the oratorical work.

11.1 That the work of oratory regularly and characteristically
creates structures of attitudes to propositions is indeed self-
evident: that it does so follows from its being polemical
and argumentative in character, and to say this is jejune. To
examine, however, the closeness between the analogue to
P_4 and the analogue to P_5 is not jejune. One example must
suffice.

11.2 Disraeli, on the *First* Reading of the 1866 Bill, had asserted that (I) it was wrong to introduce a representation of the people bill without introducing a re-distribution of seats bill to go with it and make the government's whole intention explicit. *John Bright*, in his *Speech on the Second Reading of the Representation of the People Bill, 23 April 1866*[6] (D), replied to this argument as follows: (II) to introduce a re-distribution of seats bill such as conforms to (I) means to introduce a bill which may reasonably be expected to last as long as the representation of the people bill is expected to last. But (III) in 1859 Disraeli had himself introduced a sweeping representation bill, and at the same time a re-distribution of seats bill which affected fifteen seats only. (IV) Such a bill could not possibly be expected to satisfy (II). Therefore in 1859 Disraeli himself had not believed I.

11.3 Ignoring the distinction between 1859 and 1866, the notation gives:

a. O [I]
b. $II \cdot III \cdot \rightarrow \cdot O$ [~ I] $V \downarrow O$!   (by 7.4(ii))
c. i.e. O [I ~ I] $\cdot V \cdot \downarrow O$!
d. i.e. $\downarrow O$! $V \downarrow O$!

Disraeli, either unconscious of the implications of his actions or inconsistent in his views, is descredited. *But*: if the opening assumption of 11.3 is not made, the position is that Disraeli has changed his mind, and that a proposition about which a man can change his mind is very much open to question.

11.4 The logic-and-feeling complex is thus more complex than has previously been argued: there is a kind of unstable balance and equipoise between the tendency of the argument to $\downarrow$ Disraeli, and its tendency to call I in question. One need not, therefore, be in the least surprised that Bright's references to Disraeli in this part of his speech are (though ironical) to some extent sympathetic. 'Gentlemen opposite . . . would be a great deal wiser if they remembered some of the things which the Member for Buckingham tells them' (p. 359a); 'he distributed [the seats] in a way which I am willing to admit was very fair and reasonable' (p. 360b).

11.5 The example has as its purpose to show how the analogue in the oratorical work to P_5 is regularly and characteristically 'co-

6. John Bright, *Speeches on Questions of Public Policy*, London, 1869, pp. 354–70.

adunative' with the analogue to P_4: just as P_4 and P_5 themselves refer to co-adunatives in the literary work.

III

12.0 P_6 regularly has its analogue in the oratorical work.

12.1 P_6 makes two assertions (about the presence of themes, about their being present in a distinctive manner, viz. their embodiment in details); and that an analogous postulate holds in respect of the oratorical work is self-evident. It will therefore be supported only in brief and for a particular purpose.

12.2 In the oratorical work, the analogue to 'theme' is 'principle'. It is this which the speech as a whole is based upon, and which controls its development and its treatment of detail. The guiding principle or principles of the speech need barely be explicit, and certainly they may also be embodied implicitly in the train of thought and enacted in the local detail of how it is conducted.[7] Sometimes, however, they become fully explicit; and this is no contrast with literary–imaginative works (critics regularly stress the implicitness of the theme in these, but usually also find quotations which state it). Examples are:

i/ Gladstone, *Speech in the Amphitheatre at Liverpool, 6 April 1866 (E)*: 'I ask what *justice* it is that we can ask the working population to pay us from two-sevenths to three-sevenths of the taxation, and to pay them in return with . . . one-seventh of the representation?'

ii/ *D* : 'Sir, I think that this House should be a *fair* representation of the people of this country . . . so arranged that every person of every class will feel that his interests are fairly represented.'

iii/ *B* : 'I want to show that this measure is not founded upon any calculation of results, but in broad sweeping *principles*, having their rise in the assumed rights of man!'

iv/ Disraeli, *Speech on the Second Reading of the Representation of the People Bill, 27 April 1866*: 'I hold it [the English (sic) constitution] to be a polity founded on distinct principles . . . I hold our Constitution to be a monarchy, limited by the *co-ordinate authority* of . . . the Estates of the Realm.'

7. A particularly clear example is Disraeli's speech entitled 'Conservative and Liberal Principles' in *Speeches*, ed. T. E. Kebbel, London, 1882, ii, 523–36. I discuss this in detail in *Disraeli: Speech at the Banquet . . . on June 24, 1872*, ed. H. Viebrock (*Studien zur Rhetorik des 19 Jhdts.*, Franz Steiner, Wiesbaden, 1968.)

12.3 Needless to say, the embodiment of principles in the detail of illustration and argument is a major principle of organization of material in the oratorical work (refer to 6.1) and the most definite and conspicuous aspect of its self-consistency (refer to 3.2, P_1, but also to 3.3, A_1). But although this is to begin with a matter of logic, it is certainly not rigidly confined to logic, as may be seen in the examples (12.2). 'Justice', 'fairness', practical calculation, and sense of balance (especially of balance co-ordinated over a period of time since 'the Plantagenets', which is Disraeli's base-line) are easily traced in tone, characterization, descriptive detail, irony, and other distinguishable dimensions of the feeling-structure of the oratorical work.

12.4 The more suggestive line of thought lies actually in the opposite direction: in considering whether, in view of the over-whelming prominence and centrality in the oratorical work of the analogue to 3.2, P_6, and in view furthermore of the fact that what has been said hitherto does not obscure that fact, *there is a major distinction still to be made* between the oratorical and the liter-ary–imaginative.

12.5 P_6 has perhaps been over-stressed in respect of the literary work. (Refer to 1.0 (ii).)

12.6 No assertion has been made in 12.4 and 12.5; they put forward an idea for review. But it is worth reviewing, in the light of the 'major distinction still to be made', which was referred to in 12.4. This major distinction is as follows: in spite of the existence of the analogues between oratorical and literary–imaginative already discussed, such oratory as has been discussed here, and perhaps parliamentary oratory at all times, may have substantial, or even something approaching major, literary interest, but all the same it can barely be seen as among the supreme literary forms. Yet if this is so, it is unlikely that what seems to be its character-istic principle of organization should be very like (even if not identical with) any characteristic principle of organization (see P_6) in the supreme literary forms.

13.0 I now speculate, briefly, as to what it may be in parliamentary oratory that precludes its reaching supreme greatness as literature. It cannot well be its involvement simply in *detail*. This may be unavoidable for it, but on the other hand the novel makes no attempt to avoid detail. It might be that the kind of detail involved in oratory requires special study if it is subsequently to be mastered, and that therefore even supremely great parliamentary oratory is of necessity a comparatively recondite literary taste. But that is not the point at issue. Nor does it seem adequate to suggest that it is the wrong kind of detail, in that it is generally found boring or becomes irrelevant. These would be facts too contingent to serve as bases for saying that a certain *genre* seemed to be essentially precluded from greatness; and could also be applied only too easily (indeed, have been sometimes applied) to authors like Dante and Homer. I therefore note, in particular, two other features of the oratorical work as follows.

13.1 *The work of parliamentary or public oratory is circumscribed by involvement in controversy.*

13.2 In the oratorical work, characterization, dramatization, logic-and-feeling structure, and perhaps much else, tend *necessarily* (not contingently) toward a limiting and crudifying *bi-polarity*. They need not, of course, be exclusively such: in *E*, for example, Gladstone has a substantial development both of his opponents, and of his principal topic, which is the working class. But the tendency is necessarily, not contingently there; and once made, the point is plain and pervasive enough to invite pondering without being elaborated. The inadequacy of anything like bi-polarity in criticism of supreme works should be recalled at this point. *Othello* is not all light and dark, and not even *Pericles* is all storms and music.

13.3 Moreover, organization upon the particular bi-polarity of controversy introduces a restriction of attitude and emotional range which cannot be called contingent, even if it is not clearly necessary. It is hardly right to say that the fact that there tends not to be controversy in charity, or in rapture, is a contingent fact.

13.4 The second of the two features (refer to 13.0, end, and 13.1) is that the work of oratory is circumscribed by involvement in 'the actual', in reality.

13.5 It should be noted that 'involvement in reality' is not the same thing as 'involvement in detail' (13.0). Treatment of reality may avoid detail (philosophy, metaphysics), and clearly some detailed products of imagination, though doubtless not all, are unrelated to reality. But the point is that for Lowe, say, but also for his opponents too, 'calculation of results' can never be very far away. The point is analogous to the distinction Aristotle made between poetry and history. The great work of literary art is more than a *speculum vitae*: but beyond that, it is also more than an *organon vitae*, and organization of reality comprehended and structured into its principles. To see Aristotle's 'what could be', 'what might be', fully expounded, means to see human reality within the larger and stranger perspective of human possibility, potentiality, even mystery. Put it another way: the House of Commons, doubtless, is realist; but the novel, even the novel, is ultimately not.

> *Lemma to 13.5*: There is a sense in which possibility, potentiality, and mystery, as 'going beyond' reality, are also 'part' of reality.

VEY MEMORIAL LIBRARY